"This process is destined to expand the traditional division of the sales team into hunters and farmers by adding a new category: the trapper.

—GERHARD GSCHWANDTNER the founder and publisher of the world's leading sales magazine - *Selling Power.*

"...it's all about executing a strategy that makes it easy for a customer to say "Yes"! This book provides a straightforward path to sales success and I highly recommend it."

—RICK LaDUCA, VP of Sales - The Americas, Spirent Communications

"...if you want to sell anything to anyone. Read this book and then...Sell! Sell! Sell!

—TIM DRAPER, Founding Partner, Draper Fisher Jurvetson.

"If you are trying to grow sales and do so with maximum efficiency? It can't help but improve your results!"

—DALE NEILLY, Vice President Sales and Marketing, Radiant Communications

iUniverse, Inc.
New York   Bloomington

SHiFT!
Harness the Trigger Events That TURN PROSPECTS INTO CUSTOMERS

iUniverse books may be ordered through booksellers or by contacting:

iUniverse
1663 Liberty Drive
Bloomington, IN 47403
www.iuniverse.com
1-800-Authors (1-800-288-4677)

Because of the dynamic nature of the Internet, any Web addresses or links contained in this book may have changed since publication and may no longer be valid.

ISBN: 978-1-4502-4007-9 (sc)
ISBN: 978-1-4502-4008-6 (ebk)

Printed in the United States of America

iUniverse rev. date: 6/14/2010

TABLE OF CONTENTS

ACKNOWLEDGMENTS

From Craig Elias:

Thanks to the thousands of business leaders, entrepreneurs, and sales professionals who helped me to perfect my craft by applying elements of Trigger Event Selling™ to their sales efforts.

A special thanks to my parents who taught me the importance of persistence, my son Liam who has taught me the power of having a greater purpose in life, and my wife Heather, to whom I will always be indebted, for her incredible patience during the almost three years it took for this book to come together.

Projects like this book are the result of a team of people who come together to achieve a common goal. Thanks to Tibor for his contributions, keeping me focused, and making sure this book gets out on time, and the countless others who helped make this book a reality.

From Tibor Shanto:

I would like to thank the following people in helping me make this book a reality. First and foremost my wife and family who tolerated endless nights of me banging away at my keyboard. Craig for prodding and pushing me just enough to inspire me to get the right material together.

My clients who have trusted me, challenged me and added to my expertise. All the sales people I have trained who ask me things that forced me to gain a deeper understanding of sales success. I would also like to thank Brandon Toropov, David Gargaro and Paul Simon.

Finally, all the readers, and especially, all those who regularly take time to comment on my blog (http://sellbetter.ca/blog) and newsletter The Pipeline.

INTRODUCTION

Once upon a time there was a cubicle. It might have been the one next to yours.

A salesperson showed up for work one day, entered his cubicle, and found a magic lamp that he knew for sure had not been there the day before. There was an intriguing handwritten message on a Post-It Note affixed to the lamp: RUB ME.

The salesperson rubbed the lamp briskly, and watched in amazement as a Genie appeared. The Genie swirled around in a haze of purple and green smoke, and then asked, "WHAT IS YOUR COMMAND?"

The salesperson thought for a moment, and then said, "I want to be the world's best prospector." The Genie nodded in obedience and granted the wish; ten years later, the salesperson retired.

Eventually, a new salesperson inherited the cubicle. This second salesperson also found the lamp, saw the note, rubbed the lamp briskly, and watched in awe as the Genie materialized and orbited in gusts around the room. "WHAT IS YOUR COMMAND?" asked the Genie.

The second salesperson gave this some thought, and then

said, "I want to be the world's best closer." The Genie again nodded and granted the wish; five years later, the salesperson retired.

A third salesperson inherited the cubicle, and that salesperson also encountered the lamp, read the note, and followed its instructions. The Genie materialized, circled the room, hovered in front of him, and asked, "WHAT IS YOUR COMMAND?"

Instantly, the third salesperson replied, "I want to reach every prospect at exactly the right time!"

The Genie smiled, nodded, and vanished. That afternoon, the third salesperson initiated—and one week later closed—the biggest deal in his company's history. He kept closing huge deals for weeks and months on end, shattering all records at his company.

He retired within twelve months of his encounter with the Genie.

Moral: In sales, TIMING IS EVERYTHING!

Can you remember the last time you were in front of a highly motivated buyer at just the right time—and the sale almost happened by itself? Was your skill set better than it normally is when you closed that deal? Or was your timing better?

What if there was a process that allowed you to repeatedly get in front of the right person at exactly the right time? What if you could spend most of your time talking to people who were approximately five times more likely to buy from you than people you're probably talking to now?

This is what SHiFT! is all about. It's a new way to look at selling. It is about mastering the art and science of timing. It's about SHiFTing your attention from things like prospecting and closing to things like the *Trigger Events* that make it more likely that someone will be highly motivated to buy from you.

SHiFT! is not a magic lamp with a Genie inside—but it's as close as you're going to get.

SHiFT! is a result of years of real-world experience by two sales veterans who have succeeded on their own, and have now collaborated to bring you this unique approach that will help you to deal with one of the key underpinnings of success in B2B sales: timing. Everyone acknowledges that if they can improve their ability to connect with the right buyer at the right time, their results would improve.

SHiFT! gives you exactly that—the power to harness timing, the power to anticipate timing, and the power to increase your closing ratio while reducing the time it takes to close a sale now. Unlike the story of the Genie, there is no magic in this book (unless you count the increase in sales you will experience as magical). What you'll find is a clearly laid out roadmap to things you can do to improve your timing and improve your ability to get ahead of predictable events so that you can leverage them by being there first. What you will find is the collective result of years of experience and success by two leading sales practitioners.

Between the two of them, Craig and Tibor have half a century of B2B selling experience. They have each received numerous awards for sales success, and have led their respective teams to consistent results. Nevertheless, when they first met, each was convinced that their own approach was different if not more sound. Fortunately, while their approach to sales may not have seemed compatible to start with, they got along on a personal level and the dialogue continued. As evidenced by this book you are holding, they soon discovered that their sales approaches and philosophies were not that far apart.

This book is the result of their collaboration and work to bring these approaches together in a way that leverages their respective and collective experiences. As the reader, you have the benefit of the combined outcome. Together, they present you with the philosophy, processes, and action steps needed to replicate the successes they have had. They bring together their individual and collective experience to help you improve your timing in sales and harness the power of *Trigger Events* to close more prospects more quickly and more consistently.

Did you ever have a friend or a work associate where part of the relationship was a testimonial to the old saying, "opposites attract"? One of the things you probably noticed was that what first seemed to be evidence of the difference, after examination and much debate, turned out to be not that different after all. That begins to describe how this book came together.

While Craig and Tibor did have their differences, it turns out they were based on the details rather than the big picture. After a lot of debates and discussions, they discovered that when they looked at the underlying philosophy or means of achieving objectives and results, things turned out to be much more in common than they first thought. Tibor and Craig first met in 2007 as a result of Craig reaching out to his network to find sales experts to participate in the Corporate Sales Challenge in Calgary. Someone in Craig's network knew someone in Tibor's network, and that led to their first discussion.

Before they met, Craig had a 20 year track record of being been a top performer for every company he worked for. Craig had also won a $1 million prize in Tim Draper's Billion Dollar Idea Pitch Competition for a Trigger-Event-based company called InnerSell. When Craig became a first-time father at the age of 42, he left InnerSell (which had been moved to San Francisco to collect the prize) to focus on being a great dad.

Upon his return to his hometown of Calgary, Alberta, Craig received numerous calls to share his Trigger Event Selling™ knowledge with entrepreneurs and sales teams. He started a company called Shift Selling Inc. and began doing that on a part-time basis so that he could focus on being an active dad in his son Liam's life (hence the term Dadpreneur, which was often used to describe him). Since launching Shift Selling Inc., Craig has worked with entrepreneurs and companies throughout North America. He has helped them to increase their sales effectiveness by viewing and interpreting markets based upon *Trigger Events*. He has shown them how to combine this *Trigger Event* view with unique practices that allow sales teams to create and focus on the opportunities they are highly likely to win. As a result Craig has validated his Trigger Event Selling™ methodology in numerous real-world Business-To-Business (B2B) settings.

Tibor founded Renbor Sales Solutions after a long, successful career in selling B2B services and products, including currency, financial services, and online information. Before starting Renbor, Tibor spent ten years with Dow Jones & Company in progressively more senior roles including

Director of Sales Strategy and AVP of Client Solutions. It was during these last two roles that he not only honed his sales outlook and philosophy, but was able to test it in various regions across the globe and in many different sectors.

By the time Craig and Tibor began sharing their views on selling, they had both been able to test, validate, and refine the philosophies, methods, and tactics shared in this book. This is one of the key advantages of this book. It offers equal portions of What, Why, and How. Many sales books will have the What and Why, while many others will have the How without telling the reader Why. This "works for me, so just do it and it'll work for you" philosophy was one reason that Craig and Tibor committed to offer all three elements needed not only for success, but to develop an ongoing process for improvement to keep up with the increasing demands made on sales professionals. To further this, and to provide ongoing support, they invite you to visit the book's Website at www.TriggerEventBook.com.

There you will find more resources, examples, and tools to help you continue developing what you learn in the book and leveraging the events you'll face when you start harnessing *Trigger Events* in your sales efforts.

In many ways, how Craig and Tibor came together on this book was a result of timing and doing what is outlined in the book. The more they worked together and shared each others' approaches, the clearer it became that combining their methodologies would produce something that was truly greater than the individual parts. You be the judge.

To learn more about Trigger Event Selling™, or to have Craig or Tibor speak at your company or industry event, about how to harness or create *Trigger Events* to capture new customers or prevent *Trigger Events* to keep customers longer, you can reach them at:

Craig Elias

E-mail: Craig.Elias@ShiftSelling.com
Phone: +1.403.874.2998
Skype: Craig.Elias

Tibor Shanto

E-mail: Tibor.Shanto@SellBetter.ca
Phone: +1.416.822.7781
Skype: TShanto

BEFORE YOU BEGIN...

When you try something new, it always feels uncomfortable at first. But if you do it often enough, before you know it, it becomes second nature. Let us give you an example.

Take just 10 seconds to grab a pen and write (not print) your full first name and last name using your wrong hand. In other words, if you're right-handed, use your left hand; if you're left-handed, use your right hand. Write your full name with your opposite hand in the space below.

_____

How did that feel? If you are like most people, it felt a little uncomfortable and frustrating; it probably took a fair bit of concentration and effort. It may also look like something you would have done back in Grade 1 or 2.

Now write your full first name and last name using your usual hand in the space below.

How did it feel the second time? If you're like most people, it probably felt like second nature. It was automatic, and took no thought, effort, or concentration.

What made the difference between the two experiences?

Some people say, "Practice!" Others say, "Genetics!" We disagree. It's not practice or genetics that makes the difference. It's repetition. Practice happens in a "safe" environment; it's like tracing your name with tracing paper. Repetition is what happens in the real world.

You can practice selling to your dog, but you won't have the personal "ah-ha moments" and epiphanies that occur when selling to real people, making mistakes, and course-correcting with actual prospects.

It's repetition that helps us learn things that are new and different. In this book, we'll be sharing a lot of new and different things about selling. Don't practice them. Repeat them with prospects— over and over again—in the real world.

We want you to experience this because the first time you try to apply what you learn in this book it will feel like you are writing with the wrong hand. All you need to do to improve is repeat, repeat, repeat, and soon it will feel like second nature, just like writing your name with your regular hand.

Don't worry; we will be with you the whole way. Throughout the book, we will share tips, advice, and tools to help you along, and additional useful information is included on the companion Website (www.TriggerEventBook.com).

And once you finish this book and want to know how to create *Trigger Events*, so you can push aside your competition, or how you can prevent *Trigger Events* from happening to your customers, so you keep your customers longer, you can read the two books that are scheduled to follow this one.

If you don't want to wait, you can reach out to us and we can share with you what's in the upcoming books.

Now let's begin...

If things get tough and you need some inspiration along the way, perhaps a quote by Wade Cook can help:

"If you will do what most will not do for just the next few
years, then you can do what they cannot do
for the rest of your life."

CHAPTER 1

The Window of Dissatisfaction™

"The two most important requirements for major success are: first, being in the right place at the right time, and second, doing something about it."
~ RAY KROC, FOUNDING CEO, McDONALDS

If you don't read this chapter, you will miss out on the following:

1. Knowing what your biggest competition is

2. Identifying exactly the right place at the right time in sales

3. Learning which decision-makers are most likely to buy from you in the near future

1.1 IT'S ALL IN THE TIMING

Selling, like life, is *all* about timing. This book is about timing and understanding the events that trigger timing (*Trigger Events*) and harnessing them to close more sales sooner. It's about mastering the art and science of getting in front of the right person at *exactly* the right time—which we call the **Window of Dissatisfaction**™— and then doing the right things when you have timing.

Knowing that *Trigger Events* result in highly productive sales efforts and deeply loyal customers will help you to close sales sooner and take home a much bigger commission check. Once you understand this timing—and it's easier than you think—you can learn to take the *right* action based on the decision-maker's buying mode. You can enjoy a much higher close ratio than you're experiencing right now, on bigger deals that close much more quickly, so you can move on and start selling to someone else more quickly.

The secret to being successful in sales is perfecting your timing. That means getting in front of the right person at *exactly* the right time.

To do that, you must understand the power of something that has a dramatic impact on the sales cycle, which most salespeople don't spend enough time understanding. It's called Path Dependency.

1.2 PATH DEPENDENCY

Path Dependency is what happens when decision-makers have done the same thing in the same way for so long that it's easier for them to keep doing the same things the way they have always done them. Most of the time, when you are selling, this is your competition—unless there is a compelling reason to change and a Trigger Event that makes them want to change right now.

All salespeople face the same competition: the prospective buyer's predisposition to keep doing exactly what they are already doing.

When decision-makers have Path Dependency, the investment of time, money, energy, or attention they've already made in something prevents them from taking a different approach. Just think of the way you type using a standard QWERTY keyboard (which is named after the first six letters in the top row of a keyboard). Most people have been trained to type using that keyboard layout. Why is that?

We all type that way because, on the earliest manual typewriters, the keys kept getting stuck when people typed too fast. The QWERTY keyboard was actually designed to keep the keys from jamming the mechanism! The problem is that people wanted to type faster.

The Dvorak Simplified Keyboard (shown below) solved that problem. It allowed people to type faster without the keys jamming.

However, people had invested so much time in learning to type with a QWERTY keyboard that they did not want to forgo the investment they had made or reinvest their time, money, and effort in learning something new. This is the power of Path Dependency: almost everyone is still typing on the QWERTY keyboard to this day!

The real challenge, and the real competition, is that buyers think they don't have a problem. They're happy with the Status Quo. They are too busy doing what they're already doing (i.e., taking care of things they're used to taking care of) to look at what you have to offer. Initially, it seems as though, no matter what you do, you just can't get their attention. That's the effect of Path Dependency. Once we are used to doing something, it's a lot easier to keep doing what we've always done.

Think of it this way: You have a car that you like driving, and have had generally good experiences with it over the years. On your way home from work one night, the transmission breaks. You have the car towed to the local garage, and the next day, you learn that it will cost $400 to fix the transmission. Do you buy a whole new car or do you pay $400 to fix the transmission?

If you're like most of us, you'll pay to fix the transmission. Why? Because buying a brand new car is a big undertaking, and it connects to a lot of variables you don't particularly feel like dealing with right now. Plus, you already have a good set of experiences with the car you're driving. So you fix that one. In fact, if something else goes wrong with the car in several months from now, you'd probably *still* pay to repair the vehicle rather than buy a brand new one. Sometimes, it takes a pretty dense combination of things going wrong for us to start thinking about the major commitment, such as selecting, financing, and purchasing a brand new vehicle.

> ***Your true competition is not a competitor who provides a similar product or service.***

It's the path the buyer has become used to traveling. And yet, what would happen if that person decided, for whatever reason, that the Status Quo was no longer sufficient? What would happen if you could get in front of the decision-maker on the day this happened? How would that affect your ability to make a sale and build a rewarding long-term relationship?

1.3 SEE THINGS DIFFERENTLY

If you want to improve your close ratio, you might upgrade your presentation and closing skills.

If you wanted to increase your total opportunities, you might upgrade your prospecting skills.

If you wanted to increase your deal size, you might target

different customers or sell different products and services.

But if you want to improve all these things at the same time, you would have to improve your timing. You could probably use some assistance with understanding and upgrading your timing strategy. This means you will need to SHIFT your focus, and SHIFT your tactics, so that you can SHIFT your results.

You must understand the benefit of finding buyers while they are in a powerful selling window called the Window of Dissatisfaction. Learning to see and sell to those buyers in the Window of Dissatisfaction is not a matter of slightly improving upon something that you're already doing. It's a matter of seeing the selling process a little differently than you see it right now, and consistently taking action on what you learn.

Figure 1.1

1.4 TIMING AND BUYING MODES

It does not matter what you sell or to whom you sell it, buyers are always in one of three different buying modes. If you've been selling for more than a month, you already know about two of them. However, one of those buying modes, the Window of

Dissatisfaction, may seem less familiar to you. Let's look more closely at all three buying modes now.

1.4.1 *Status Quo*

On one end of the spectrum is the familiar Status Quo mindset. This is when the buyer has Path Dependency and believes that the current solution meets his or her needs. It's like being on a moving train where the tracks are pointing you in only one direction.

Here, the buyer sees absolutely no reason to change. This is the part of the continuum where the person says to you, "It's okay, we're happy with what we have." In other words, the buyer will keep buying whatever he or she is already buying from the current supplier.

Decision-makers will stay in Status Quo and keep buying from their current supplier until something triggers a change. This mode is good if you're the established vendor the person is buying from but not so good if you're a salesperson on the outside trying to get in.

Think of the decision-makers in this buying mode as happy and not searching for any alternative solutions. You've run into your share of those people, right?

1.4.2 *Searching for Alternatives*

Most salespeople are equally familiar with the other end of the spectrum, which is Searching for Alternatives. At this stage, buyers clearly understand that the solution they have no  longer meets their needs. They have chosen the type of solution they want and are actively engaged in the process of Searching for Alternatives when It comes to potential suppliers of that solution.

Think of decision-makers in this buying mode as unhappy and actively searching for an alternative solution. Have you met those kinds of people in your capacity as a salesperson? Of course. The only trouble is, by the time you meet them, some other salesperson has already gotten the first-mover advantage and has the inside track. The buyer has already defined *the solution*—and often, that definition effectively precludes your offering. Still, the decision-maker may tell you to "send a quote." Why? Because due diligence requires him or her to talk to multiple vendors. Does that mean you get the deal? Usually not.

1.4.3 Window of Dissatisfaction™

What many salespeople don't realize is that between these two commonly known buying modes is a third buying mode,

 which isn't quite as obvious as the other two modes—until you learn to recognize it.

This buying mode typically requires a little practice for salespeople to learn to see.

That practice, however, could be the best time investment you ever make in your sales career. If you are a professional salesperson, you should know that understanding and learning to see this most important buying mode, the Window of Dissatisfaction, is the key to putting timing on your side.

Think of decision-makers in the Window of Dissatisfaction as unhappy but not searching for alternatives... yet!

It is during this powerful selling window, before the decision-maker takes action, that he or she has begun to see different ways to solve the problem. This is where real opportunity can be found. The decision-maker's buying cycle typically starts long before we start our selling cycle. **The Window of Dissatisfaction is where the decision-maker's buying cycle starts.**

The Window of Dissatisfaction opens as a result of events

that trigger people to forgo their Path Dependency and start thinking about doing something different. Notice, though, that it opens *after* the buyer experiences a Trigger Event that causes them to leave Status Quo but *before* that buyer has found the time to start the process of Searching for Alternatives.

This point is critical to your sales success so we are going to say it again. If you take nothing else away from this book, remember this:

The Window of Dissatisfaction begins after the decision-maker experiences a Trigger Event and decides that what he or she has is no longer sufficient, but before he or she has started doing anything about it.

The following visual will help you to put this career-changing point in perspective.

Figure 1.2

Happy	Unhappy	Unhappy
with Status Quo	with Status Quo	with Status Quo
Not Searching For Alternatives	**Not Searching** For Alternatives	**Searching** For Alternatives

1.5 TIMING AND SALES CYCLES

If you've studied marketing, you're probably familiar with the AIDA (Attention, Interest, Desire, Action) formula for what you want to do with your promotion and marketing efforts. In our case, we looked at it from the decision-maker's point of view and what they go through.

The process of what people go through before they make a purchase becomes:

A = Awareness I = Interest D = Desire A = Action

Think of the Window of Dissatisfaction as being comparable to the Desire (D) stage in the AIDA formula.

When you find buyers in the Status Quo buying mode, you have to wait for them to go through all four stages, which is usually a very time consuming process.

When you find buyers in the Window of Dissatisfaction, there is already an *Awareness* of a problem, there is already *Interest* in solving the problem, but most importantly an event has triggered the *Desire* to leave Status Quo and start thinking of ways to solve the problem. However, there has not been any *Action* to solve the problem yet.

Basically, what's happening in the Window of Dissatisfaction is that the buyer has experienced a *Trigger Event*. (Chapter 2 is all about understanding these *Trigger Events*.) That *Trigger Event* has put something important on the buyer's to-do list, but the buyer is busy and can't find the time to do anything about that to-do item yet. You can identify with this, can't you? We all know what it's like to get so busy that you can't do everything you'd like to do.

When you're a buyer, and you're in the Window of Dissatisfaction, you know that you *should* be taking action, but you're just so busy with everything else that you haven't been able to get around to doing it yet!

Buyers in the Window of Dissatisfaction speak a special language, which takes just a little time for any good salesperson to master. Later in this chapter, we'll show you how to understand that language. For now, though, we'd like you to think for a moment about what *usually* happens when salespeople don't bother to understand that language.

Those salespeople typically end up doing one of two things:

A. They speak to people who haven't begun the AIDA process and are not yet aware of a problem - aka Status Quo.

B. They speak to people who have already completed the AIDA process and have decided on a course of action that involves a competitor - aka Searching Alternatives.

They skip everything in the middle! How much sense does that make?

When you get to buyers in the middle they have desire or emotion related to solving a problem they are most likely

to act. By focusing on these buyers, you'll have a much shorter sales cycle, a higher close ratio, and you will sell at a much higher price.

1.6 TIMING AND CLOSE RATIOS

Here's a question. How much do you think it is costing you—in terms of both time and money—to talk to prospects and customers the way typical salespeople do?

In 2003, as part of his research for his first company InnerSell, Craig surveyed more than 200 sales managers and salespeople around the world. Out of that research came some numbers we are going to share with you. The numbers vary by industry and geography so we'll give you the range of typical numbers.

As it turns out, when you are trying to sell to someone who's in Status Quo buying mode (the buying mode where the person is "satisfied with what they have"), your close ratio is likely to be less than 1% (1 in 100). That's a lot of time, and not a lot of dollars. And that's not such a surprising number when you think about it. Remember, people in this buying mode are happy with what they have, and see no reason to change.

When you find buyers who are on the other end of the spectrum, in the Searching for Alternatives mode, the numbers get a little better. The odds are between 10 and 20% (about 1 in 5, 1 in 6, or 1 in 7) that you will close the sale. There are a lot of variables, of course, but on average that's what you'll be looking at.

Why isn't the number higher than 20%? Because these people have realized that what they have is not sufficient, and have already chosen the preferred solution. At this stage, they are going through the motions with different suppliers. ("Send me a quote!") Of course, when someone is already talking to a number of different suppliers, it reduces the odds of your closing the deal.

When you reach people while they are in the Window of Dissatisfaction, and you get to them before anyone else does, your average close ratio will be between 60% and 90% (on average, about 75%). Why is the close ratio so much higher? Because they want to solve the problem but have not yet taken action on selecting the solution they will use.

Think about that for a second. On average, **you are five times more likely to close a sale when you have the right timing**. "Right timing" means that you are the first viable seller to see this decision-maker while they are in this Window of Dissatisfaction. You are five times more likely to close that sale than you are when you reach the same buyer once they have moved into the Searching for Alternatives buying mode.

Again, it's all in the timing!

1.7 TIMING AND VALUE

Your close ratio is so high when a decision-maker is in the Window of Dissatisfaction because that is when they typically see the most value in becoming your customer. Let's look at the three buying modes more closely now, this time in chronological order and with the perspective that a decision-maker generally pays more when they believe they are getting more value. As shown in figure 1.3 below, a buyer's perception of value changes as they go through the three buying modes.

Figure 1.3

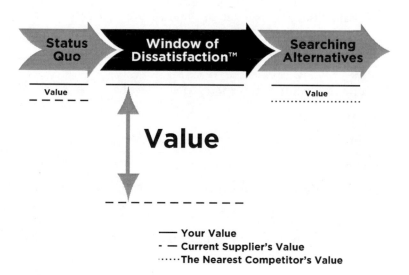

Status Quo

Let's say that you find a buyer during the Status Quo buying mode, as shown in the preceding diagram. The dashed line represents their perception of the value of what they currently have. The solid line represents their perception of the product or service that you provide. The challenge is that, during the Status Quo buying mode, the difference between the two lines is typically not enough to convince somebody to become your customer.

Window of Dissatisfaction

But then something happens. You know what that something is, don't you? It's a *Trigger Event*. Maybe a provider unexpectedly closes up shop for a week or misses a deadline. Maybe there's a quality problem or a change in personnel. It could be any one of a thousand things. But something happens in the buyer's world, something triggers a new way of looking at the situation, and suddenly the buyer's level of satisfaction with their current solution decreases.

Now that the buyer has entered the Window of Dissatisfaction, their perception of the value you provide is far greater.

Searching for Alternatives

But there's a challenge. If you do not connect in time with the buyer who's in the Window of Dissatisfaction, and that buyer starts the process of Searching for Alternatives, their perception of value becomes the difference between what you offer and what your nearest competitor offers! This is the difference between your dashed line and the competitor's dotted line.

Obviously, you want the buyer to define your value before your competitor enters the picture. You want to reach the buyer before they start talking to your competition and the Window of Dissatisfaction closes!

1.8 TIMING AND THE BEST CUSTOMERS

Once you grasp this concept of value, you realize the importance of reaching the buyer while they have the problem on their to-do list but before they have started compiling a list of alternate suppliers.

Why is timing so important? When you find a buyer who is still in the Window of Dissatisfaction, you tend to get a much higher price than you do when the buyer has begun Searching for Alternatives. Once that search begins, you get a much lower price. Similarly, when you find a buyer in the Window of Dissatisfaction, you tend to get a very short sales cycle, as opposed to a very long sales cycle once the buyer begins Searching for Alternatives.

By the same token, your close ratio is generally very high in the Window of Dissatisfaction compared to when you find someone who is already Searching for Alternatives. Then, your close ratio is very low.

This is why this new understanding of timing matters!

A buyer's perception of the value you bring changes according to the buying mode you find them in when you first start selling to them. The buying mode you find somebody in also has an impact on the kind of customer that person turns out to be.

Figure 1.4

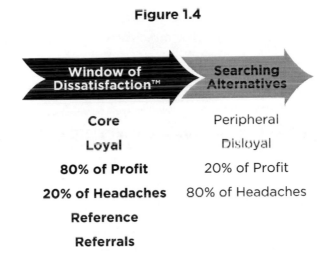

Window of Dissatisfaction™	Searching Alternatives
Core	Peripheral
Loyal	Disloyal
80% of Profit	20% of Profit
20% of Headaches	80% of Headaches
Reference	
Referrals	

As shown in the figure 1.4, when you find a buyer in the Window of Dissatisfaction buying mode, you will tend to find a core, loyal customer who will represent 80% of your profit and 20% of your headaches. These types of customer will gladly be a reference for you and are likely to pass along timely referrals, one of the most treasured things in sales. Our experience has been that buyers who are Searching for Alternatives, on the other hand, tend to be peripheral, disloyal, unprofitable, demanding customers. These buyers are unlikely to be a reference for you and unlikely to give you referrals.

It comes down to this: **The sooner you get in front of these motivated buyers, the more likely you are to become the person that helps them shape what they believe to be the ideal solution to their problem.**

In the previous figure 1.4 above, the customers we all want are on the left. The ones that most salespeople get are on the right. The only difference is how soon you got to them during their buying process.

1.9 STOP DOING WHAT YOU'RE TOLD!

How do you take advantage of timing? By learning the language people speak when they are in the Window of Dissatisfaction. This is a language that very successful salespeople have learned to use. Fortunately, it's not that hard to learn because you speak this language yourself when you're a buyer.

Let's look at how you can understand when people are in these different buying modes, and what you should do when you find them there.

1.9.1 *Status Quo*

As we said earlier, you probably have a very good sense of when a buyer is in Status Quo buying mode. Here, buyers will generally say, "Sorry, Craig, I'm not interested. I don't need it right now." Typically though, the person will not say, "We don't need that and we never will." The message is, "We really don't need what you're offering right now." Whatever they've got up and running—whether it's a relationship with a current supplier or some other way of handling their situation—is working for them. Your timing is not right because they're all set for now.

1.9.2 *Searching for Alternatives*

Now let's fast forward to the third mindset, Searching for Alternatives. This is one you have to be careful of, as it sounds so enticing. When you talk to these people, you feel like you've finally succeeded! The person says, "Craig, I'm so glad you called. This is exactly the right time for us to be talking about this. Tell me all about what you're offering." You may even hear, "Send me a quote as soon as possible!"

Even though these kinds of messages can sound very encouraging, especially after you've received ten or twelve rejections in a row—and even though you want to spend time with these people—building relationships with them should not be your top selling priority!

Why? Because they're almost certainly talking to multiple prospective vendors right now, in addition to talking to you. What's more, they already believe they know what the ideal solution looks like! When you spend all of your available time jumping through hoops for these people, your deals will be smaller, your selling cycle will be longer, and the lifetime value of the customer will be smaller than you deserve. That's what happens to most salespeople because what they hear initially from buyers who are Searching for Alternatives sounds more encouraging than anything they initially hear from people in the other two groups. All that glitters is not gold.

To move to the next level in your career, you have to set your sights on identifying that group of buyers in the middle, the critical group that's still in the Window of Dissatisfaction.

1.9.3 *Window of Dissatisfaction*

You're probably curious: How can you recognize these people? Well, as we say, it takes a little practice. Often, these people will say things like, "I'm really busy, but can you call me back next week?" It almost sounds like a brush-off because they usually are, like the rest of us, really busy. In fact, most of the time, salespeople treat that response as though it were a brush-off because they won't set a date and time to get back in touch. But with practice, you will learn to recognize something in the person's tonality that suggests he or she does want to talk to you at some point.

These buyers may say, "You know what? I'm going to be looking at that in a few months. Why don't you call me back in September when we'll be looking?" It's now July; they're telling you to call back in September. They could have simply said no, or even hung up on you. They didn't. They want you to stay on the radar screen. Why? Because they have something on their to-do list, which they know they should take care of. They're thinking that you can help them take care of it. These are the people you want to build up relationships with! Why don't they want to talk about it right now? You just interrupted them, and they have a lot of things to do. That's all.

These are the people you want to connect with!

When you hear something like, "Call me back in September," they are really saying, "I want to talk to you at some point." Bells should start going off in your head. And whenever you hear those bells, you should know that, at that moment, your only job as a salesperson is to focus like a laser beam on this opportunity. Learn as much as you can during this first call, follow the buyer's lead, and then find creative ways to not have to wait 60 days (or whatever it was) before getting back in touch.

You do not have to follow the buyer's instructions in the Window of Dissatisfaction! You do, however, have to follow the person's emotion and intent.

1.10 REACH OUT NOW!

Read it again! The person said you weren't supposed to call until September... or next month... or three weeks from now... or whatever the "instant timeline" he or she created when you interrupted the day. Ignore that.

You must find some way to get the Window of Dissatisfaction buyer out of the mental environment that they are in during your first call, which is likely to be "wrap this call up quickly." You must find some way to connect with them again—the sooner the better, regardless of the instructions you were given!

You may now be conditioned to call people back when they tell you to call back. Recondition yourself!

---

*Change this part of your selling routine
and you can change your career!*

Take the buyer out for breakfast, coffee or lunch, golf or skiing. Or, if you're far away, try to set up a conference call using CynoCast, Go To Meeting or a similar service. Whatever the person told you to do, change the pattern somehow and find a way to get back in touch in the short term. (In Chapter 4, we will share specific ways of doing this in a way that the prospect will respond to positively.) Doing this will accelerate the pace at which the prospect will confide in you their "dissatisfaction," and lay the groundwork for you becoming the Emotional Favorite™.

To make that happen you must get them out of their office (an environment where they are likely to be interrupted by a phone call, email, a superior, a co-worker, or a subordinate) so that the Window of Dissatisfaction buyer can tell you more about the problem, preferably before the end of the week.

Don't get too hung up on timelines, but do get hung up on the idea of getting this person engaged, sooner rather than later, no matter when you were told to call back. Your goal with the buyer in the Window of Dissatisfaction is to have a friendly conversation about the problem, whether that's on the first call or the second. It's best if this happens during the first call, but even if it has to happen during the second call, you can still plant a few seeds about what your solution looks like. And you can get the buyer to walk away with the understanding that you might be able to address this issue that's been bugging them, but that they haven't yet been able to do anything about.

Don't be fooled into thinking that calling back a couple of weeks before September (or whenever they told you to call) will make any difference. All you will be doing is wasting time while the person moves into Searching for Alternatives mode—where your competitors will be ready and waiting!

1.11 HAS IT HAPPENED ALREADY?

If you have been in sales for a few years, you probably have a few customers you reached while they were in the Window of Dissatisfaction. But do you know which ones they were?

Would you like to know which of your current prospects are currently in the Window of Dissatisfaction?

Set aside 30 minutes and you will understand
EXACLTY who are the best prospects
and how you can get to them.

During that 30-minute period, take the first 10 minutes to use the form in figure 1.5, that is found at www.TriggerEvent-Book.com/window, and make a list of the new customers you've acquired in the last 12 months.

Figure 1.5

Customer Name	Situation			
	Shorter Sales Cycle	Easy	Higher Price	Reference-able

Start with your newest customers (the ones you recently won) and work backward. If you have too many to cover in half an hour, then pick the top five or ten (i.e., the ones who matter most in your world). Identify as many people who have bought from you for the first time within the last 12 months.

Once you've made that list, identify the ones where you had a shorter sales cycle. Put a checkmark next to each of those where you had a shorter than average sales cycle.

Next go down the list putting a checkmark next to each of those people you feel were easy to sell to.

Next, put a check mark beside the customers where you encountered little or no price objection.

Finally, put a checkmark next to those people who you feel are more than willing to be a reference for you.

Now look at all the people who have three or more checkmarks next to their name. In all likelihood they were in the Window of Dissatisfaction when you first connected with them.

If you're like most of the people we work with, getting to this point of the analysis will take you no more than ten minutes. For the balance of the 30 minutes you set aside to do this exercise, try to identify the best possible answer to this question: What exactly did you do to find these specific customers? Invest time and attention figuring that out. Replay all the scenarios.

Focusing on the answer(s) to that question with great internal clarity, day after day, will help you to put the power of repetition on your side and help you to notice when you are facing a situation where a decision-maker is likely to be in the Window of Dissatisfaction.

What you have just done is a form of Won Sales Analysis™. This is an extremely important tool that will help you replicate your biggest wins. We cover a more detailed form of Won Sales Analysis™ in Chapter 3.

1.12 DO THE RIGHT THING

When you start interacting with prospects, you're going to notice that something very interesting is happening. You'll notice that, just like you, buyers have something called Selective Perception.

Most of the time, the buyer's Selective Perception is looking for evidence to stick with what's already working. That's just the way human beings are programmed. We don't usually go around trying to change systems and habits that aren't giving us a problem. We operate on the assumption that there's no real problem, and we look for evidence to support the idea that there's no real problem.

Most people you talk to are looking for evidence that they don't really have a problem. In these cases, Selective Perception is operating on behalf of your true competition in the sales cycle - Path Dependency. As we've seen, this is the routine that has already been built up—the sheer force of habit—that connects to sticking with an existing vendor (or no vendor at all).

Because they're looking for evidence that they don't think they have a problem, most people are happy with the Status Quo. They are too busy to look at what you have. And no matter what you do, you just can't get their attention. They have Path Dependency. As described earlier in the chapter, they're happy with what they have, and it's a lot easier to keep on doing what they've always done than it is to do something different.

Changing what we're doing right now to address a business problem involves Path Dependency. In most cases, unless there's a major problem, we don't want to go through the headache, hassle, and hard work of establishing a new vendor relationship. If there's an existing relationship that's working, then it's okay. Sometimes, doing nothing is okay.

You always have competition, but the competition is not a person or company. The competition is not a competitor who provides a similar product or service. It's the path the buyer has become used to taking.

Your competition is the Status Quo, which is all the different ways they can use to get the same outcome, or solve the same problem while spending the same money. It may not necessarily be the same amount, but it involves spending the same money.

So what do you want to look for? I guarantee that you will see four or five times more people in the Window of Dissatisfaction when you look for buyers who are dissatisfied with your competition, not just your competitors.

So let's put this all together...

When you find buyers in Status Quo buying mode, they are happy with what they have and see no reason to change. The long-term strategy here is to become the buyer's Emotional Favorite, which is the person they would rather do business with, and find a way to raise the buyer's expectations. As long as the buyer's perception of the current supplier's product or service is greater than or equal to the buyer's expectations, they will stay in Status Quo buying mode.

When you find buyers who are actively engaged in Searching for Alternatives, you must find a way to reduce the buyer's perceived risk of being your customer. The majority of buyers act in a risk-avoidant way. They already have a preferred choice, or a favorite. And odds are they will not change. But the idea is if something happens and their first choice falters, we want to be their *clear* alternative choice. And you want them to buy from you because they think it's less risky than it is to buy from any of your competitors in that situation.

When you find buyers in the Window of Dissatisfaction, your only job is to get them out of their office and telling you about the problem they want solved or the outcome they would like to achieve. Let them talk and, when the time is right, plant a few seeds around how you can help them.

The big question is: How much time do you want to spend

with those buyers? Wouldn't you rather spend your time with the people who've made an internal commitment like this?

"Man, I've got to start looking for a new car. This is the fourth time this car has gone into the shop in the last five months."

SHIFT!

There are three key things to take away from this chapter:

1. YOUR BIGGEST COMPETITION IS buyers who have Path Dependency. These buyers in Status Quo buying mode have a lot of time and money invested in what they currently have and are happy with the value they get from their current solution.

2. PERFECT TIMING IS when the decision-maker has entered the Window of Dissatisfaction, and no longer believes that what they use provides sufficient value. They want to do something about this but they are too busy Searching for Alternatives related to other time-sensitive issues that they are not talking to your competition.

3. YOU KNOW YOU HAVE TIMING WHEN the buyer tells you about the problem they want solved or the outcome they want but they do not tell you the exact solution they want to buy.

Actions

To take advantage of what you now know, you should do the following:

1. Spend at least 50% of your prospecting time with those who are in the Window of Dissatisfaction.

2. Get those who say something like, "Call me three months from now," out of their office and talking about the problem now, not two or three months from now.

3. Review every sale to get a feel for what a decision-maker in the Window of Dissatisfaction looks like and the actions they typically take.

Resources:

- A full sized (8.5 X 11) version of the Window of Dissatisfaction worksheet and a completed example can be downloaded from www.TriggerEvent-Book.com/window

- Special offers on Sales 2.0 tools and services related to the Window of Dissatisfaction, such as Cyno-Cast can be found at www. TriggerEconomy.com

CHAPTER 2

Trigger Event Selling™

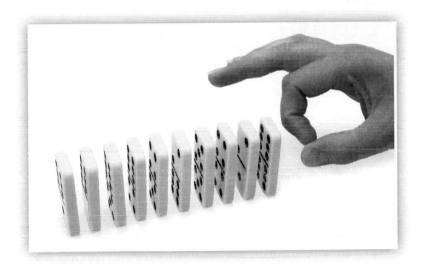

*"You have a row of dominoes set up, you knock over the first one,
and what will happen to the last one is the certainty
that it will go over very quickly."*

~ DWIGHT EISENHOWER

So how can someone be in Status Quo on Monday and then in the Window of Dissatisfaction™ on Tuesday? The answer is simple: the person experienced a *Trigger Event*.

If you don't read this chapter, you will miss out on the following:

1. Why your target customers can want what you sell all of a sudden

2. How to start seeing the *Trigger Events* that create customers everywhere you go

3. Three things that make target prospects want your products and services

2.1 TRIGGER EVENTS

We have all seen clips on the news where someone decides to set a new world record with an exhibition of falling dominoes; as they fall, the dominoes create an elaborate picture. Everything is in place, all the angles are perfect, but nothing happens until one event sets off a chain reaction of events. One tipped domino creates all of that movement! It is the same in selling.

Thousands, even millions, of dominoes are lined up in your prospect's world... and then one thing comes along and changes everything. That one thing is the *Trigger Event*. Planning and being ready will help you to leverage and take advantage of the *Trigger Event*. Without preparation, you may become a spectator to the opportunity instead of the person who benefits from it.

What goes into a *Trigger Event*? Read the following true stories. As you read them, consider how many times you have seen something similar unfold in your world. Think of all the decisions you made due to a single event—your personal *Trigger Event*.

Because we want you to internalize what we are talking about, on occasion we will provide you with two examples: a B2B example that applies to your selling efforts and a B2C example that applies to your personal life. It is our intent that one or both will resonate with you and you'll have a better understanding of what we are talking about.

2.1.1 Changing the Product Mix

Acme International, a sales organization, had a tightly focused line of products that were sold on a subscription basis. Territory reps were incented on two metrics: closing new streams of revenue (i.e., capturing new logos), and maintaining and growing the monthly recurring revenue (MRR). The sales reps had a Customer Relationship Management (CRM) program in place to manage the business; each rep managed his or her plan through a spreadsheet process that allowed them to communicate where they were against the plan, determine their commissions, and so forth. Managing and administering the compensation plan and payouts was relatively simple; using that compensation plan to motivate the team and drive performance was also straightforward, due to the relative simplicity of the product line and the plan.

Then a new and innovative CTO came on board, a host of spin-off products materialized, and suddenly each salesperson had an opportunity to offer new versions and components of their core products. This was good for the reps and the company, as it allowed them to get into more companies, expand their presence in existing accounts, enhance their role as the incumbent, and leverage the Status Quo.

However, new products also added some complexity; the margins on the company's products now varied wildly, which impacted the payout to the sales reps. It required the company to move from a simple compensation plan based on a single percentage of revenue payout model to a variable plan with different permutations based on what was sold. In addition, the new products led to the recruitment of specialists (people who sold only one product), which had a further impact on the administration and management of the compensation plan.

For a number of years, the CRM account executive who sold to Acme had been looking for ways to upsell different components to the company. One day, while sitting with the Sales Operations manager, he heard her express apprehension about the following week, which was the quarter end. Commission and bonus payouts had to be calculated and submitted to finance by the following Friday. Given all the new products, commission arrangements, and team members, she knew that it was going to be a nightmare.

At that moment, the CRM rep recognized a *Trigger Event* had occurred. The addition of new products that shook up the existing compensation scheme allowed him to demonstrate and quickly sell the company the Incentive Manager add-on to his CRM program, which simplified reporting.

2.1.2 *The Broken Phone*

Craig had been a loyal Dell customer since 1992, a loyal Palm Pilot user since 1998, and a loyal Nokia cell phone user since 2001. (That's called Path Dependency!) He'd gone through all the different versions of Palm Pilot—from the original Palm Personal to the Palm LifeDrive. And then, one day his Palm LifeDrive died. (That's another component called circumstance change. You'll learn more about each of these ideas shortly.) The death of his Palm Pilot, however, was not a *Trigger Event* because Craig had just bought a new Dell XPS mini-laptop. Once his Palm Pilot broke, he decided to make do by just using his recently acquired laptop and his familiar Nokia cell phone for a while instead of going through the trouble, expense, and time investment of resurrecting a new Palm

Pilot. This laptop-as-database approach was fairly easy, since the Palm database was already synchronized with his Outlook contact database in the laptop.

But then Craig noticed something. Every time one of Craig's contacts changed cell phone numbers—which was a fairly frequent event because he has so many contacts—an interesting sequence of events would play out. A contact would call from a new cell phone number; which put Craig into the habit of entering the new cell phone number into his trusty Nokia instead of the (unavailable) Palm Pilot. Soon, the Nokia became a data island: the only place where all the updated cell phone numbers could be found. (That's a new situational problem—an incremental change in circumstances.)

In the back of his mind, Craig knew that he should do something about this situation, and he put this problem on his mental to-do list. He needed something to integrate his contacts. Addressing that problem wasn't much of a priority for a couple of months. Then, one day, something happened. The first iPhone came out to huge media fanfare. Was that a *Trigger Event*? No, as it didn't cause Craig to discuss plans with anyone or take any action. All the launch did was create an awareness of a potential solution. There needed to be a *Trigger Event* for Craig to justify taking action.

Craig decided that he wanted a new iPhone, but he already had a Nokia phone that he couldn't justify throwing away and he could not give it to his wife because she already had a reliable flip phone. Then came the *Trigger Event*, the tipping point, the moment of truth: Craig's son Liam, who was two-and-a-half years old at the time, snapped his wife's reliable flip phone in two.

Why was that the *Trigger Event*? Because now Craig's wife needed a new cell phone, an event that got Craig thinking again about Apple's new iPhone. He had a brilliant idea. He went to his wife and said, "Hey, sweetheart, what do you think about this? You can have my cool Nokia cell phone and I'll get myself an iPhone."

She went for it!

2.2 THE TURNING POINT

Up until the point at which an event triggers action, people will keep doing what they've always done. They will stay on the path they are already on. Even though they might be unhappy with some aspect of what they're facing, they will most likely keep doing what they have always done. That's the power of the force of habit engrained in the buying mode of Status Quo. There is usually an investment of time required to address a new issue properly, and there is also something else that's more pressing for us to do. So we fall back into our routine and stick with Status Quo.

The *Trigger Event* is what gets people to think about doing things a little differently. Once your son snaps your wife's phone in two, you start thinking, "Hey, maybe it's time to do something about that problem." Once you have a dozen new products, and a dozen new problems related to figuring out commissions for your sales team, you start thinking, "Hey, maybe we should look at a new way to put together our end-of-quarter numbers."

What would the conversation have been like if an Apple iPhone salesperson happened to call Craig within 24 hours of his son breaking that flip phone? How easy would that sale have been?

By the same token, what would the CRM salesperson's outcome been if *some other* CRM supplier had contacted that client with a solution for managing end-of-quarter numbers more seamlessly and easily? Could a new vendor have gotten a foothold in the account? You bet!

Remember: Sales is all about timing!

Look closely at what we have shared thus far with you about *Trigger Events*, and you'll see the three powerful concepts that will help you to identify people who eventually find themselves in the Window of Dissatisfaction™.

2.3 WHAT COMES BEFORE THE WINDOW OF DISSATISFACTION™?

The three elements that precede any Window of Dissatisfaction are:

1. Status Quo (Path Dependency);

2. An incremental change in circumstances that creates the pain;

3. The *Trigger Event* that makes a decision-maker more motivated to deal with that pain.

Let's look at each of these three elements individually.

2.3.1 Status Quo (aka Path Dependency)

No matter what you sell or to whom you sell, the buyer you are targeting always has an existing way of solving the problem or getting the desired outcome. This is the Status Quo, which includes all the different ways of addressing the issue at hand, not just the competitor who is an alternate provider of the same product or service that you provide. The Status Quo could be doing nothing. Too many salespeople fixate on a single competitor but lose sight of the larger issue of the *true competition*, which is the Status Quo.

For example, Bob is looking to buy his wife a gift for a

special occasion: an anniversary. Once Bob has become use to buying flowers in a certain way for such special occasions, he tends to stay on that particular path.

If you run a jewellery store, another jewellery store may be your competitor, but your real competition is Bob's Path Dependency: his habit of buying flowers for special occasions like anniversaries.

2.3.2 *Incremental Change in Circumstance*

As salespeople, we have been trained to focus on the buyer's pain, but we sometimes forget that the pain is just a circumstance. We do not really want to know whether the buyer is in pain, but whether the pain is sufficient for the buyer to become motivated to do something about it now.

In the "incremental change in circumstance" mindset, the pain has not yet been translated into action. We know we have a problem but we put up with it because our motivation to solve the problem is less than the effort required to solve it. You may tell yourself, "I have other more pressing items that I am more motivated to resolve." The emotion related to the situation has never become intense, or if it ever was intense, it has diminished to the point where the buyer lapses back into Status Quo mode.

For instance, suppose you've become used to living in a certain house or apartment, even though you know you could do better. For some people, the time and effort of finding a new place and moving into it is just not worth initiating—at least not until some other event comes into play.

Consider the parable of the frog and the pot of boiling water.

You put a frog in a pot of water. You then put the pot of water on the stove and turn on the heat. What happens to the frog? Because the temperature rises slowly, the frog gets drowsy, falls asleep and ends up getting boiled. But if you bring the water to a boil first and then put the frog in the pot, the frog will quickly jump out. Because the change happens during a shorter time frame, the frog notices the difference and takes immediate action. Any series of incremental changes in circumstance in the buyer's world is like that water that slowly comes to a boil. It doesn't produce immediate action.

Trigger Event

Figure 2.1

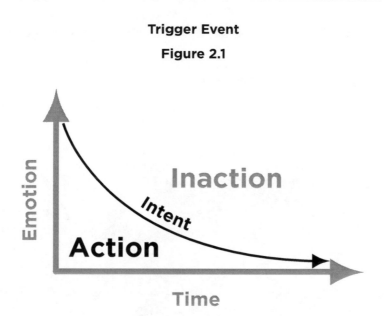

VS.

Incremental changes in circumstance

Figure 2.2

2.3.3 *The Trigger Event*

Something has to happen that disrupts the pre-existing pattern we've created, or makes it difficult (or unwise) for us to follow that pattern any more. This "something" is the *Trigger Event*.

For example, your fiancée tells you that the relationship is over if you don't find a better place for the two of you to live. Or the transmission in your car gives out, and you realize that you have to think seriously about replacing the car you've been meaning to replace for the last year and a half. Suddenly, you move from not having the time or energy to look at your options to realizing that you can't keep doing what you've always done.

Let's look at an example that will illustrate how this *Trigger Event* principle works on the organizational level. For years, Telus and Bell, each a dominant player in wireless phones In Canada, took different strategies when it came to technology from their competitor Rogers. Rogers was an early adopter of SIM card-based phones, allowing it to be compatible with the dominant technology through most of the world – GSM, Bell and Telus continued with their CDMA platform, even as the rest of the world was moving to GSM and SIM cards. Were there downsides to this strategy? Sure. Until 2007, Bell customers had to make alternative arrangements for wireless whenever they traveled outside of North America. This meant lost revenue from business travelers when they were overseas, and defections from clients who did not want to deal with the hassle. Other downsides included a lack of the latest and shiniest handsets like the iPhone, and lost roaming revenue from foreign travelers coming to Canada from overseas. The upside: a large percentage of their customer base traveled only in North America, and since they shared a technology platform with the largest carrier in the U.S., both Telus and Bell were able to effectively compete for a large part of the pie.

But in 2009, both Telus and Bell decided to make substantial investments (reports indicated that it was more than $500 million) to upgrade their networks to a SIM card-based platform. Was it the lust for the iPhone? What triggered their decision to build out the network, even though they would have to maintain their old network into the future? The answer: the 2010 Winter Olympics in Vancouver. This meant an influx of tens of thousands of foreign visitors and athletes, all carrying SIM card-based phones, and all generating a lot of roaming-fees. For Telus and Bell, the Winter Olympics and the potential of a significant amount of roaming fee revenues constituted a mandate for sudden and radical change: it was a *Trigger Event*.

Although a *Trigger Event* doesn't necessarily lead to immediate action, it does lead to a change in outlook. This is the event that triggers a new sense of urgency for us—a challenge to create a new plan of action. Once we've entered this phase, we're open to considering a new way of doing things... even if we may not have taken any action on the problem yet.

For instance, you might think that the *Trigger Event* that connects to a married man's decision to buy the prescription medication Rogaine would be easy to identify: going bald. Actually, the married man who's going bald may not yet have had a *Trigger Event* that will change the path that he is on:

going balder. So, what's the *Trigger Event* that's likely to lead a married man to get a prescription for Rogaine? Getting a divorce and becoming single again!

One of the things we have to understand about *Trigger Events* is that, as a general rule, the emotional intensity of the desire to change will diminish as time goes along.

Figure 2.3

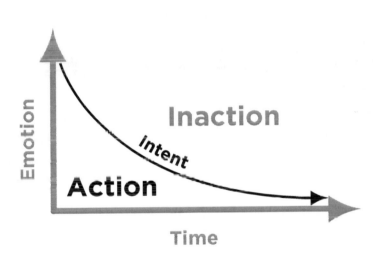

This is the Law of Diminishing intent.

When decision-makers experience a *Trigger Event*, they have a lot of emotion related to solving the problem. This emotion it transferred to intent, but the problem is that it dissipates over time.

What is the big difference between a change in circumstance and a trigger event? Time.

Jack, a businessman, had been a mid-level manager at the same company for the last eight years. As a manager, he was not required to wear a suit to work, and he made a habit of shopping for "business casual" clothing. One day, his boss told him that, a week hence, a very important client would be paying a visit on-site. There would be a plant tour, followed by some critical negotiations where Jack would be involved.

Figure 2.4

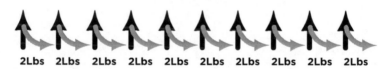

2Lbs 2Lbs 2Lbs 2Lbs 2Lbs 2Lbs 2Lbs 2Lbs 2Lbs 2Lbs

Jack's boss also said, "By the way, Jack, you'll need to put on a suit that day. This client places a lot of importance on dressing for success."

That night, Jack went home and pulled out his old "power suit," which had always seen him through big meetings back in the day. It was a lucky thing he tried it on when he did because the old suit, lucky or not, was more than a bit too tight. Because Jack had slowly put on weight, and not worn the suit for years, he was not aware of the incremental change in circumstance. The act of getting ready for the meeting triggered a new imperative: Jack either had to lose 20 pounds in a week (not very likely) or buy a new suit. Result: He bought the new suit.

When something happens over a period of months or years, the emotion is experienced in very small increments. The smaller the increment, the smaller the emotion behind solving the problem. That's the big difference between a change in circumstance (which Jack had been experiencing for eight years) and a *Trigger Event* (which he experienced when he was preparing for the meeting).

2.4 WHERE DO YOU WANT TO BE?

Think about all three of these preconditions, and then think about the one that is most difficult for you as a salesperson to work within the prospects you encounter.

Is there really any doubt? It's Path Dependency.

Status Quo (Path Dependency), the first of the three mindsets we've shared, is extremely powerful. If people are in Status Quo buying mode, they won't see the opportunity that your solution brings, and they'll be too busy to look at what you have to offer. No matter how hard you try, you'll find it difficult to get on their to-do list until they experience a *Trigger Event* (or a series of *Trigger Events*) and shift into the Window of Dissatisfaction.

That's the moment when they become highly motivated buyers. That's when you want to reach them... when they are motivated but have not started the process of Searching for Alternatives.

2.5 TRIGGER EVENTS AND MOTIVATED BUYERS

The sooner you get in front of someone who is motivated, the more likely you are to win the business.

Sometimes, as we suggested above, one *Trigger Event* does not create enough emotion or intent to solve the problem. These decision-makers languish in the Window of Dissatisfaction until they drift out of it because the emotion dissipates and they don't have enough intention to find the time in their busy schedule to take action.

But then along comes another *Trigger Event*. Let's say that this one is powerful enough to spur action in the short term. What will happen? Perhaps the decision-maker starts the process of Searching for Alternatives. Even then, decision-makers have been known to stick with what they have if it takes too long to find a suitable solution. For such buyers, it might take a third or fourth powerful *Trigger Event* to create a strong enough intent for them to buy something else. Once they do, they have created a new Status Quo.

Whenever someone experiences a *Trigger Event*, that person has a new item on his or her to-do list. They know they have to take care of it, but it's still down their list of things to get done. The *Trigger Event* motivates the buyer, starts the buying process, and prompts the buyer to notice all the different ways there are to solve the problem, a phenomenon known as Selective Perception.

When you talk to a motivated buyer before your

competition, you get to help shape what the newly motivated buyer believes to be the ideal solution. Suddenly, that buyer compares their current solution to yours and they are not very happy with their current solution. It works because you help to create a new or revised Status Quo.

The buyer now thinks they have a solution to their problem. It turns off their Selective Perception, which is covered more in Chapter 3. Thanks to the *Trigger Event,* and your ability to recognize and capitalize on it, you're the means by which the buyer begins taking action on the problem.

2.5.1 *The Credible Resource*

What happens when someone is in the Window of Dissatisfaction, is motivated to buy, and runs into a credible resource that can help to solve the problem? Very often, that prospective buyer begins talking to someone else in his or her inner circle about the interesting discussion they had with that credible resource. If you do the work necessary to become the credible resource driving that inner-circle discussion, you've got the inside track!

Once buyers believe they have found a candidate for the ideal solution, they take the problem off their mental "radar screen" and breathe a sigh of relief. When the time comes for the buyer to make a final decision, your competitors are likely only to get cursory attention and the buyer is likely to maintain an attachment to your solution. Why? Because you're the one who has defined the parameters of both the problem and the solution. As a result, you and the *Trigger Event* have created the new Status Quo, a new Path Dependency. Of course, the buyer is very likely to stay on that path until a new sequence of incremental changes in circumstances creates both pain and a new *Trigger Event* that renders that pain unbearable.

2.6 THREE TYPES OF TRIGGER EVENTS

What events will motivate buyers to see your solution in a new light? What will have them seeing value in taking your call? What will lead them see value in your solution?

To answer these questions, you should know more about the three different types of *Trigger Events*. Remember: we're not looking for circumstances. We're looking for events that typically fall into one of three specific categories.

There are three different categories of *Trigger Events*:

1. Bad experiences

2. Changes or transitions

3. Awareness events

2.6.1 *Bad Experiences*

Here, the buyer has a bad experience and becomes unhappy. This type of event happens on the current supplier side of the equation. Specifically, something happens to disrupt or undermine the buyer's relationship with the current supplier. For the most part, this experience begins with an unexpected and unpleasant change in a product or service. The bad experience may be with the product or service used by the buyer, the people the buyer deals with inside the company, or a large-scale problem in the company.

If you can recognize and harness the opportunity, created by a bad experience, you can become the buyer's new Status Quo and start that person down the path of buying from you.

Here's a hypothetical example. Mrs. Baker's Cakes and Pastries Ltd. had been using Marshall Transport to deliver their products for years. They have had a good relationship with Marshall, one based on trust, service and reliability. Price was not the driving force in the relationship.

Senior executives at Mrs. Baker's Cakes were particularly pleased with the cleanliness of Marshall's trucks. They felt that the trucks' appearance and drivers' professionalism added to their company's positive image in the market. Then the global recession hit, and Marshall, like all businesses, began looking for ways to tighten belts and reduce costs.

Management at Marshall's made the decision to extend the service life of their trailers from four to six years. While safety was never compromised, maintenance of the equipment was now driven more by economics and regulatory commitments than it had been in the past.

While Marshall's trailers were as sound as ever, they began to show their age. Still, the relationship with Mrs. Baker's was steady— until the Vice President of Marketing at Mrs. Baker's had a phone conversation with a buyer at one of the major chains. The buyer had not called to complain but in the normal course of conversation he asked, "Hey, did you guys switch trucking companies?"

The VP said no, they hadn't, and then said, "Why do you ask?"

"Nothing specific," the buyer said. "The deliveries are still on time, but the trailers look a little more tired, a little less crisp than they used to. I thought you may have switched."

Next Monday at Mrs. Baker's executive committee meeting, guess what was on the agenda? You guessed it: What to do about the image problem with shipping to that major chain.

Within a week, Mrs. Baker's was talking to Gord's Transport, who had been regularly calling on Mrs. Baker's for the past few months. Gord's Transport won the contract to ship to the chain that brought up the issue, and all other shipment routes came under review.

A few weeks later, when the VP of Marketing was talking to the buyer, the buyer mentioned that he was pleased to see that Mrs. Baker's had taken his input and acted to fix the problem.

2.6.2 *Changes or Transitions*

The second type of *Trigger Event* is a change or transition. This happens on the buyer's end of the equation. It is typically related to a change in people, a change in places, or a change in priorities in the buying organization. It could be a change in the people who do the work, or a change in the people who make decisions about how the work gets done. By the same token, it could be a change about where the work gets done or where the decisions about how the work is done are made. It could even be a change in a decision-maker's priorities. Regardless, the changes are internal to the buyer's environment. Unlike the first category of *Trigger Event*, this one is not about the current supplier, but rather the buyer.

You know this scenario. You have an account you want to get into, but the competition is entrenched in the account and no matter how often or how hard you try, you can't get in. Then, one day, the buyer or decision-maker at the account changes. Suddenly, resistance disappears and, before you know it, you have yourself a new customer.

The opposite is also quite common. You have a relationship with a decision-maker, and that relationship allows you to enjoy the benefits of having the "inside track" on a lot of new projects. Then, one day your reliable contact leaves and you lose the business to someone else!

A change in place can be a change in location for an

organization. Changes in location—such as a headquarters move—are a great opportunity to get prospects off the track of doing things in one familiar way. When the surroundings change, the perspective can change, too.

With a change in priorities, there's often a change in management and a change in that management's organizational aspirations. When the management team changes, the organization's priorities usually change, too. That's another great opportunity to go in and make your case with a prospect that previously had a state of Path Dependency with your competition.

Consider the following B2B example. In a series of actions taken to deal with the recession, Acme Manufacturing decided to consolidate its two California locations under one manager, who prior to this had only managed San Francisco. He had always been a loyal Red Brass Bearings customer, while Los Angeles had always used West Coast Supplies. With the new management and a focus on savings and consolidation, the opportunity for Red Brass has changed for three reasons:

1. A change in the location where a decision is made

2. A change in the person making the decision

3. A change in priorities to lower cost

Something like this is like the "Perfect Storm." When there are multiple *Trigger Events*, the decision-maker needs to act with even more urgency that when there is just one.

2.6.3 *Awareness*

The last kind of *Trigger Event* is a new awareness of something. This event is created by something the prospect sees, hears, or reads about. These events typically happen as a result of an action taken at your end of the equation. It's not a bad experience, and it has nothing to do with internal changes at the buying organization. It's a new perspective of their current situation.

Many salespeople try to create such an event by promising that what they have is better, faster, or cheaper. But in most cases, there is not enough emotion involved in the "better, faster, cheaper" message to get the decision-maker to move this item up the to-do list. The information that tends to create the greatest sense of urgency relates to legal (statutory or regulatory) requirements or risk avoidance.

After legal requirements the biggest single awareness event that gets people to act is a new awareness of risks they face if they don't act. When this happens they ask themselves questions like, "How do I keep what I have?" or "How do I avoid missing out on something in the future?".

For example, let's say that you sell advertising and you try to get one of the top three car manufacturers to advertise in your magazine. Individually, each of the decision-makers perceives the purchase as too risky and don't buy. Then you learn that there's a change in personnel at one of those companies, which means a change in priorities. The new decision-maker decides to advertise with you. Suddenly, the other two car manufacturers want in because they become aware that their competition is in your magazine and they risk losing sales to their competition.

2.7 WHAT TO LOOK FOR

Your job now is to determine the top three changes or transition events within your customer base—the events that create a Window of Dissatisfaction and an opportunity to sell your product or service. Those are the events you are really looking for; those are the events you want to learn to recognize and act on.

A lot of salespeople waste precious time and energy trying to spot and capitalize on bad experience events or trying to create an awareness event. These are strategic mistakes because:

- Bad experience events are nearly impossible to predict;

- Awareness events seldom create the level of emotional intensity needed to drive change and if they do but you don't have Emotional Favorite™ status with the decision maker, the decision maker is highly likely to *borrow* your idea and give it to their Emotional Favorite™ to implement.

Bad experience events have a lot of emotion connected to them, but these events are difficult, or even impossible, to predict—though we certainly want to take advantage of them when we come across them. (In fact, when we run into them, these should be our top priority.) Awareness appeals are generally low-percentage shots. What we're really looking for is change or transition events that create the Window of Dissatisfaction.

If you're not working on opportunities where the buyer had a bad experience, then you should focus on customers that have recently experienced a change or transition.

The lowest priority should be to focus on those people you're trying to make aware of the fact that there is a better way.

2.8 PROSPECTING SCENARIOS

Here are three prospecting scenarios that connect to what you have learned in this chapter. Each is important to understand in its own right.

2.8.1 *Status Quo*

When you find someone who's in Status Quo buying mode, odds are there's been no *Trigger Event* for quite a while. In this situation, a lot of salespeople would think, "This person isn't buying; let me move on to the next person on my list."

That would be short-sighted because you could be looking at a great long-term opportunity. If the buyer has money, authority, and influence, you should consider creating a relationship with the buyer now so they phone you first when a *Trigger Event* creates the time for them to buy. (Chapter 4 is all about how to make this happen)

In many cases, your job is to phone these people once a month. When you phone, you want to know if there been some change or event that would motivate them to become your customer—an event that would move them out of Status Quo and into the Window of Dissatisfaction. You want to phone at least monthly because you want to connect with these people when they're in the Window of Dissatisfaction, not when they're Searching for Alternatives! With these monthly check-in calls, you're establishing the fact that you are reliable, persistent, and focused. You are exactly the kind of credible resource that people are hoping to find when a *Trigger Event* shifts them into the Window of Dissatisfaction.

2.8.2 *Window of Dissatisfaction*

Let's say that you're prospecting and you find someone in the Window of Dissatisfaction, as they have recently experienced a *Trigger Event*. These people may tell you they know they have a problem, and they know they should do something about it. They'll probably say something like, "Phone me back in September." (Assume that the call takes place in July.)

Sometimes we think that we're being savvy salespeople when we way to ourselves, "You know what? I'll phone that person two weeks in advance, and I'll get the edge." But the problem is that it usually doesn't work. Someone else has gotten in before you by the time August 15 rolls around! There's an important lesson here: The Window of Dissatisfaction virtually always presents you with a short-term opportunity, no matter what the prospect says!

That's why we emphasized in Chapter 1 that we want to find some way to learn more about the challenge the buyer is handling, and then plant a few seeds around what you can do to help them. Your job is to do as much as you can on the first call. Then, create ways to get in front of this person before the date you were given. Get back in touch quickly—no matter when the person said you should reach out again!

2.8.3 *Searching for Alternatives*

Now let's suppose you find someone who's Searching for Alternatives. This person has already had a *Trigger Event*, and it's happened a while ago. The buyer may have already started talking to your competitors!

Perhaps you think that this is a great short-term opportunity. It's not. It's a medium-term opportunity because the buyer has almost certainly made a first choice. Read that again: **This buyer already has a preferred supplier**—someone he or she would like to see become the preferred supplier. The best thing you can do here is position yourself as the buyer's first alternative choice and wait for the current preferred supplier to falter.

2.9 IT'S HAPPENED ALREADY!

The best way to learn to spot *Trigger Events* that happen to decision-makers in your territory is to identify *Trigger Events* that lead up to or resulted in major purchases in your own life.

Once you have the ability to reflect on your own past purchases and can identify the specific *Trigger Event* (or series of *Trigger Events*) that led to the purchases, you are now ready to take the next step and identify the specific *Trigger Events* for the products and services you sell. We'll give you a great tool for doing that in the next chapter

Before you go on to the next chapter, take five minutes to identify your own buying triggers. Use the form in figure 2.5 (found also at www.TriggerEventBook.com/trigger-events) to reflect on some of the purchases you made in your own life.

Think of the last five or ten things that you purchased and see if you can identify personal events that led up to the purchases. They could have been a change in demographics, such as how old you are, whether you're married or single, or a change in your financial situation brought on by a new job or promotion. You might also recognize these events by looking for what created a change in your aspirations, your values, or your interests.

Figure 2.5

Trigger Event Selling™

Personal *Buying Trigger* Identification

Purchase	Buying Trigger		
	Bad Experience	Change or Transition	Awareness
Car			
Will			
Stereo			
House			
Vacation			
Furniture			
Computer			
Television			
Renovations			
Cable Provider			
Phone Provider			
Financial Advisor			
Business Clothes			
Internet Connectivity			

SHIFT!

There are three key things to take away from this chapter:

1. CUSTOMERS WANT WHAT YOU SELL TODAY BECAUSE a *Trigger Event* or a series of *Trigger Events* caused them to shift from Status Quo into the Window of Dissatisfaction.

2. YOU WILL START SEEING TRIGGER EVENTS WHEN you look back at your own purchases and can identify the types of events that led up to or resulted in those major purchases.

3. THE THREE TRIGGER EVENTS THAT CREATE DEMAND for what you sell are:

   A. A bad experience with the current supplier;

   B. A change or transition inside a company;

   C. An awareness that they need to change to adhere to a new law or avoid risk.

Action

To take advantage of what you now know, you should do the following:

- Stop looking for pain and start looking for *Trigger Events* that create pain or make that pain unbearable.

- Take action as soon as you learn of the *Trigger Event*. If you wait too long, the emotion and resulting intent to do something will dissipate to the point where the decision-maker sticks with the Status Quo .

- Analyze the purchases you have made so that you can start noticing the *Trigger Events* that happen to the decision-makers in your sales territory.

Resources:

- A full sized (8.5 X 11) version of the personal buying trigger worksheet and a completed example can be downloaded from www.TriggerEventBook.com/trigger-events

- Special offers on Sales 2.0 tools and services that are related to *Trigger Events* can be found at www.TriggerEconomy.com

CHAPTER 3

Won Sales Analysis™

Learn the past, watch the present, and create the future.

~ Anonymous

Now that you know what *Trigger Events* are, and the three types of *Trigger Events*, we are going to share a strategy for winning more deals in the future by identifying the *Trigger Events* that brought you business in the past.

If you don't read this chapter, you will miss out on the following:

1. Which *Trigger Events* result in your best customers

2. What to say to get prospects to become your customers

3. How to close more sales with those who are motivated to buy now

---

3.1 WHAT ARE YOU ANALYZING?

If you are like most salespeople, the odds are good you have been spending your time analyzing the wrong thing.

Most salespeople have been trained to spend their time, effort, and energy looking at the sales they lose so that they can determine why they lost the sale and identify "what went wrong." Our perspective is different. To win more business, we believe that you need to reflect on what made you win so that you can replicate your biggest wins.

Many sales managers have been heard saying, "If you lose the sale, don't lose the lesson." We want to challenge you to do the opposite: When you win the business, learn how you can win more just like it.

This is exactly what Craig did in the summer of 2002. For many years, he just got lucky in sales. He had a knack for being in the right place at exactly the right time. This streak of luck continued until September 10, 2001, which was the day he joined a company called WorldCom. The next day, the world changed—and it kept on changing in the days that followed, especially if you sold for a living. For those of you who can't remember what it was like selling in the aftermath of 9/11, let's just say that it was extremely tough to get anyone to change their buying pattern. People were deeply entrenched in their Status Quo.

But even in a post-9/11 environment, Craig managed to get lucky again. He was named the number one salesperson in all of Canada less than six months after joining the organization. Unfortunately, that was just before WorldCom admitted conducting $11 billion in accounting fraud. The world changed again. For the first time in his life, Craig found himself in a situation where absolutely nobody would buy from him.

He had some holiday time coming. So he waited until August, and he took afternoons off for the entire month. Every afternoon he analyzed his past sales to determine when he had been good, when he had been great, and when he had been absolutely unstoppable.

That August, Craig did something he'd never done before—he reflected on his successes. By doing so, he not only learned what had created his success, but he also learned a process that he could repeat over and over again to get in front of highly motivated decision-makers at exactly the right time.

The system you are reading about now is based on his reflections during August 2002, and the insights that came from them.

At the end of August, he began to think that there must be many people who thought along the same lines, so he did an experiment. He went to Google and typed in the phrase "sales analysis" in quotes. He inserted the quotes because he was looking for just those two words in that order. Google told him that there were almost 500,000 pages on the Internet that contained the term "sales analysis." He then decided to add the word "lost" to the search; he typed "lost sales analysis" in quotes. He found more than 2,500 pages that talked about how to win more business by analyzing the business that you had lost. But that is not what he had just done. He had found a way to replicate his biggest wins by analyzing the business he had already won, not the business he had lost. And when he searched for the phrase "won sales analysis" in quotes, he found, to his amazement, only two pages on the Internet.

Of all the pages on the Internet that talked about sales analysis, **virtually none of them talked about winning more business by analyzing the business you have already won.** Craig's conclusion was that a lot of salespeople are analyzing things but almost no one is analyzing what they are actually doing *right*.

Even now, years later, when you search for the phrase "Won Sales Analysis," there are only a handful of pages, outside of those that link back to us, that talk about how to win more business by analyzing the business you have already won.

In his analysis, Craig was able to identify a specific set of events that triggered the buyer to have a sense of urgency around solving a problem. Once he did that, his own Selective Perception kicked in, and, everywhere he went, he saw the *Trigger Events* he had identified.

3.2 SELECTIVE PERCEPTION

We want you to begin doing what Craig did: start noticing the Window of Dissatisfaction and the *Trigger Events* that create them by making use of something we all experience on a regular basis: Selective Perception.

Certain events in our lives trigger changes in what we see. When we buy a new car, we start seeing that same car all over the place. When we sell that car and buy a new car, we start noticing the new car all over the place and stop noticing the old car as much. The moment women get pregnant, they and their husbands start seeing pregnant women all over the place. When they give birth to their child, they start noticing women carrying babies and stop noticing pregnant women as much.

The human mind is an amazing thing. It allows us to see

71

the things that are most relevant to this time in our lives. The right event triggers the process of Selective Perception. So the question for you should be: What *Trigger Event* will have you noticing decision-makers who are in the Window of Dissatisfaction, and seeing the *Trigger Events* that create it?

We have learned that there are three events required to make this happen:

1. A look back at business you won while the decision-maker was in the Window of Dissatisfaction, which enables you to see what a customer in the Window of Dissatisfaction looks and acts like. (Hopefully, you took the time to do this at the end of Chapter 1.)

2. A review of personal purchases so that you can identify the *Trigger Events* that resulted in the purchases you made. (Hopefully, you took the time to do this at the end of Chapter 2.)

3. A special form of *Trigger Event* analysis called Won Sales Analysis, which enables you to identify exactly which *Trigger Events* bring the majority of the business you win and the characteristics of these opportunities. (What we are going to teach you in this chapter)

By the way, if you have not taken the time to do the exercises at the end of the first two chapters, we strongly suggest that you go back and do them now. What follows in this chapter will be of much more value to you if you do.

Figure 3.1

Trigger Event Selling™
Won Sales Analysis™ Worksheet

Customer Name: _____ Date of Sale: _____
Services Sold: _____ Rating: _____

IDENTIFY			
What changes/events lead up to this purchase? (Select all that apply)			
Bad Experience	**Change**	**Awareness**	**Notes/details**
☐ People	☐ People	☐ Legal	
☐ Product\Service	☐ Places	☐ Risk Avoidance	
☐ Company	☐ Priorities	☐ Economics	

FIND
When did the event(s) happen?

CLOSE
What made you choose us?

IMPROVE
How can we make it easier to become our customer?

CLASSIFY			
Customer Demographics (Select One For Each Column)			
Size	**Decision Maker**	**Industry**	**Notes/details**
☐ < $100 Million	☐ Finance	☐ B2C	
☐ $100 Mil. $500 Mil.	☐ Operations	☐ B2B	
☐ > $500 Million	☐ Sales / Marketing	☐ Wholesale	
Lead Source (Select One)			
Marketing	**Sales**	**Self**	**Notes/details**
☐ Online	☐ Local	☐ Networking	
☐ Offline	☐ Regional	☐ Cold Calling	
☐ Channel	☐ Divisional	☐ Customer Referral	
Size of Sale (Select One)			
☐ < $10,000	☐ $50K - $100K	☐ $500K - $1Million	**Notes/details**
☐ $10K - $25K	☐ $100K - $250K	☐ $1 Mill. - $2.5 Mill.	
☐ $25K - $50K	☐ $250K - $500K	☐ Over $2.5 Million	
Sales Cycle (Select One)			
☐ < 14 Days	☐ 3 - 6 Months	☐ 1 - 1.5 Years	**Notes/details**
☐ 15 - 45 Days	☐ 6 - 9 Moths	☐ 1.5 - 2 Years	
☐ 46 - 90 Days	☐ 9 - 12 Months	☐ > 2 Years	

3.3 WON SALES ANALYSIS™

So, what is a Won Sales Analysis? It's a tool whose primary purpose is to help you see more opportunities that you are highly likely to win. It's designed to change what you notice so that you can start seeing *Trigger Events* all over the place.

A Won Sales Analysis has five main components.

1. **Identify:** What *Trigger Event* led up to you winning the business?

2. **Find:** How can you get to highly motivated decision-makers before the competition?

3. **Close:** What made the decision-maker choose you?

4. **Improve:** How can you close more sales by making it easier to be your customer?

5. **Classify:** What are the characteristics of those who are highly likely to buy from you?

Every time you win a new customer, go back to that account for a brief interview. Use the form that appears in figure 3.1 (it can be downloaded from www.TriggerEventBook.com/won-sales) to ask the decision-maker the questions across the top half of the form, making sure that you document the responses.

Then classify the opportunity based upon the checkmarks and notes in the classify section of the form. Once you have filled out a few, search for patterns in your customers, and identify your conversion rate based upon the type of leads you generate and where those leads come from.

It's extremely important to go through this process with all new customers. After the sale has been made, but before you start delivering the service, have a face-to-face discussion with the decision-maker. Don't send them an e-mail or survey form; do it in person or over the phone.

It is important to make sure that you get specific answers to *all* of the questions we are about to share with you. That may mean asking your question several times in different ways. This is why you should conduct this interview in person or on the phone. These are the best settings for getting a new customer to fully articulate the reasons for choosing you, which can be accomplished by pushing just a little bit.

Let your new customer know that you are asking these questions because it will put you in a better position to provide better service and ensure that you meet his or her expectations.

3.3.1 *Identify*

The primary Identify question is; **"What event or events led up to this purchase?"**

As the name suggests, this section of the Won Sales Analysis is designed to help you identify the types of *Trigger Events* that you should look out for. Why? Because these events result in decision-makers buying from you.

Remember: *Trigger Events* create a sense of urgency that makes solving this problem or pain a priority. They make people emotional, and this emotion gets them off the path that they are on so that they can start down a new path—the path of becoming your customer.

In other words, you want to know what made them decide to do this now as opposed to doing it three months ago or waiting until next year. The intent here is to identify the specific events that make a decision-maker motivated enough to switch suppliers and become your customer.

If you don't get the kind of response you're looking for from the primary question, ask a variation of the question. For instance:

- What changed to make solving this problem a priority?

- What created a sense of urgency around solving this problem?

- What makes the Status Quo (or: what you were using) no longer viable?

These types of questions bring us to our Satisfaction Formula. Satisfaction (i.e., the Status Quo) exists when P is greater than or equal to E ($P \geq E$), where:

P = the decision-maker's perception of the performance of the current supplier's solution.

E = the decision-maker's expectations of what a supplier and/or the supplier's solution should deliver.

A Window of Dissatisfaction is created when an event triggers the decision-maker's perception that the performance of the current solution to drop below expectations ($P < E$).

In other words, a decision-maker will stay in Status Quo buying mode as long as they perceive that the performance of the current solution or provider is greater than their expectations. When expectations are satisfied, the decision-maker stays in Status Quo. But when a *Trigger Event* suddenly occurs, the buyer perceives that the performance of their current supplier is less than their expectations and this shifts the decision-maker into the Window of Dissatisfaction.

We're emphasizing this formula because the following principle is vitally important to you as you conduct your Won Sales Analysis. You are listening for *Trigger Events* that created the Window of Dissatisfaction by either reducing the decision-maker's perception of the value of what they currently use or raised their expectations.

$$\textit{Window of Dissatisfaction} = P \leq E$$

From this formula, we can conclude that *Trigger Events* usually cause one of two things to happen:

1. A decrease in the decision-maker's perception of the performance (value) of the current supplier's solution or people

2. An increase in the decision-maker's expectations

Let's look at an example. There's a new decision-maker in one of your accounts. The previous decision-maker had a certain set of expectations, but that decision-maker left to work for another company. Now a new person comes along with a different set of expectations, and the new decision-maker's expectations are greater than your performance as the current supplier. Your account is now at risk because of the increase in expectation created by the change in decision-maker.

Because you are the current supplier, you must fix this situation quickly! By the same token, though, if you were not the current supplier, you want to **harness the opportunity quickly** before the incumbent supplier has a chance to fix it.

Now, let's say instead, there is a change in the seller's performance. As you might expect, whenever a current supplier's performance (i.e., people, product, provider) is seen to be less than the buyer's expectations, that decision-maker moves into the Window of Dissatisfaction. By the way, the one event that causes this to happen more often than any other is a change in salespeople.

What does this mean? When you take over somebody else's account, or you're responsible for transitioning accounts, you must make sure that you get a face-to-face meeting with the account's decision-makers and influencers as soon as possible so that you can ask these questions:

- "What did the last salesperson do really well?"

- "What do you wish that person had done better?"

- "What does nobody do that you wish everybody did?"

On one occasion when Craig asked these questions, an engineer at a multi-million dollar account said, "It drives me crazy when I send out an e-mail asking for assistance, and no one responds that they got the email and are looking after my problem." Craig learned that, as a result of this problem, the engineer started making the same help request to multiple suppliers just to see who would actually respond.

Can you guess what Craig did after that? He started quickly sending responses back to anyone and everyone who sent him a request for help via e mail... and he noticed that he won a lot more business as a result because he got and kept first mover advantage. In many cases, he was able to confirm that additional suppliers were not even asked for assistance!

Look at the three questions again:

- "What did the last salesperson do really well?"

- "What do you wish that person had done better?"

- "What does nobody do that you wish everybody did?"

Pose these three questions whenever you take over a new territory or inherit someone else's account.

Every time you get to a buyer who has experienced a *Trigger Event*, make sure that you understand that person's expectations so that you can then meet or exceed them—so that person will buy from you instead of somebody else!

3.3.2 *Find*

The primary Find question is; **"When did the event(s) happen?"** This section of the Won Sales Analysis is designed to help you get to decision-makers as soon as possible after they experience a *Trigger Event*. Depending on the scenario, and your ability to identify events that came before the one that created your opportunity, this section can also help you learn to anticipate *Trigger Events*... and determine which buyers you should be spending your time with now because they are likely to experience a *Trigger Event* in the near future. Remember that as soon as the event happens, the decision-maker's intention to solve the problem begins to diminish. As we know, this is why it's critical to get to the decision-maker as soon after the *Trigger Event* as possible.

Very often, the challenge salespeople face is that they get to a buyer motivated by a *Trigger Event* that occurred so long ago that the emotion related to solving the problem has diminished to the point where it doesn't justify the effort required to become your customer.

If you'd gotten there earlier, you would have had a bigger wave of emotion to ride! The timing and level of emotion are key. So, the critical question is: When did the event happen?

If you don't get the kind of response you're looking for, ask a variation of the question. For instance:

- What led up to that event?

- What decision(s) started the sequence of events that led up to the one(s) we just talked about?

- What purchases made this problem become more of a priority?

What's important to understand is that *Trigger Events* tend to make people emotional, and emotional people change their buying habits. The more emotional people are, the more likely they are to act. We want to help you find out *when* an event happened so that, when it happens the next time, you can get there sooner than you did last time—and perhaps anticipate or predict when they will happen. The closer you get to the *Trigger Event* that produces the emotion, the better your chances of harnessing that emotion while it's still strong enough to help the buyer to jump over the hurdles of leaving the present supplier and becoming your customer. If the person is not emotional enough, then they won't make it over the hurdles. It's that simple.

One of the many reasons that office supply companies moved to online ordering was to take advantage of impulse buys and reduce the consumer's effort in making the purchase. In other words, they wanted to get closer to the *Trigger Event* and harness the resulting emotion more effectively. If you suddenly need something (such as a set of markers), you may be motivated to get them. However, by the time you realize that you have to leave the office, drive to the plaza, line up to pay, and so on, you are likely to decide that you can live with things as they are or pick up the markers on the way home. By that time, the emotion has probably dissipated and you may conclude that you can do without the markers. With online ordering, it is easy to take action right after the *Trigger Event*, and the markers are usually delivered that afternoon or next day. At the same time, having learned one supplier's online order system, it will make it more difficult for the next supplier to win you as a customer because you are less likely to learn a whole new system—unless your current supplier drops the ball.

If possible, you want to be able to identify the decisions, purchases, or events that came before the one that resulted in the sale. Doing so can allow you to anticipate the events you are looking for.

Moving the order process online is a form of Demand Compression. Look at what happens: Demand for the markers is created when a *Trigger Event* takes place. Your last useable marker dried up, and you moved into the Window of Dissatisfaction. At some point, you're going to purchase a new batch of markers. The critical question is *when*.

The farther apart those two moments are—the moment the demand is created and the moment the demand is fulfilled—the lower a salesperson's close ratio will typically be. So if you can find a way to do what the office supply company does—namely get in front of somebody when they still have the demands that were *just* created by the emotion of a *Trigger Event*—you will find that people are more willing to buy something from you.

The closer you move the point of demand creation, which is the *Trigger Event* that put people in the Window of Dissatisfaction, the less likely your buyer is to seriously consider other vendors. In effect, by getting to the person early, you can create a whole new Status Quo.

3.3.3 Close

The primary Close question is; **"What made you choose us?"**

This section of the Won Sales Analysis is designed to help you understand what made the decision-maker buy *from you*. It will also help you to determine the outcome the decision-maker thought that they were buying from you, so that you can understand the buyer's current expectations and keep them in the new Status Quo and they will buy from you again in the future.

If you are fortunate enough to get to decision-makers right after they experience a *Trigger Event*, you need them to sell themselves on your solution and spread the good word about your solution to others. An essential prerequisite for doing this involves understanding *why* the sale is likely to happen in the first place. If you don't know that, you can't expect the buyer to work with you, remove obstacles for you, or help you to build a coalition for change within the enterprise. This may seem obvious, but our experience is that most salespeople don't understand the justification that buyers used to sell themselves on a given solution, and then justify the decision to their superior, subordinates or peers.

In your Won Sales Analysis, it is important to ask a "what" question, not a "why" question in this section, because "why" questions tend to make people defensive and shut down. (Which question would you rather answer: "Why are you a salesperson?" or "What made you decide to become a salesperson?")

If you don't get the kind of response you're looking for, ask a variation of the question. For instance:

- What got you excited about our solution?

- What do you see as the extra benefits of buying from us?

- What was the outcome you achieved by making this purchase?

The intent is to get beyond the usual focus on features and benefits, which is what you may initially hear in response, and understand the buyer's definition of the value of working with a supplier. Your goal is to understand the *outcome* the person expects to get by becoming your customer. That's invariably some combination of the seller's *content* and the buyer's *context*.

Salespeople typically have great content. We can tell a decision-maker the reasons it makes sense to use what we have. The buyer has to supply the context about how that content applies to them and their employer. Some buyers are able to make the connections between their context and our content with a little mental gymnastics; for other buyers, the answers don't come quite so easily. In this part of the Won Sales Analysis, a critical goal is to understand the mental process that your best (and, let's face it, smartest) customers go through in connecting your offer (the content) to their situation (the context). Once you understand how these customers "connect the dots," you will be in a better position to help other buyers come up with compelling reasons to purchase your solution.

Admittedly, pulling this off is more art than science. One's level of mastery of this art usually depends on one's depth of experience as a salesperson.

The junior salesperson trying to complete this section of the Won Sales Analysis tends to have a predetermined list of questions that they want answered. As soon as the new customer offers a cursory response to a question, the junior person moves on to the next question.

A senior salesperson tends to have a better grasp of the importance of getting a clear understanding of the meaning behind the verbal answer. As a result, these salespeople ask a special kind of follow-up question known as "second order" or second level questions. They're often invitations to elaborate on an answer, and tend to sound like this:

- Which means... ?

- And that resulted in... ?

- And so your goal was to...?

Top-performing salespeople use a completely different strategy for developing a deeper understanding of the customer's purchasing decision: **six seconds of silence**.

Once the customer you are interviewing for your Won Sales Analysis answers a question, you say nothing and count in your head to six before saying anything. This takes practice, but the act of giving the new customer six whole seconds to think about their answer can deliver remarkable insights on the underlying emotional reasons that supported the decision to buy from you.

You're probably wondering what happens if the customer waits those six seconds and says nothing to elaborate on their initial answer to your question. Do you just sit there and stare at each other? No. After six seconds have elapsed, you repeat the last few words they used with an inquisitive voice. This is a form of paraphrasing with a question mark at the end.

For example, if a decision-maker says, "I chose you because I had more faith in your ability to deliver the solution on time." Wait—don't ask your next question. Give them six seconds and if they say nothing else, then say, "On time?"

Invariably, you'll find that the customer will expand on their answer, and offer more information than if you had come back with a direct question. Remember, you're out to learn not only about the surface reasons, the logical justifications people give for buying, but the emotional reasons that support those justifications. In the grand scheme of things, emotional reasons are far more important for you to understand.

(Side note: As you may have gathered, the "second order" and "six second silence" strategies are also great tools for discussions with prospects whom you want to *turn into* customers.)

You're going to all this trouble in the Close section of the Won Sales Analysis to learn which of the five basic reasons that people buy apply to your customer.

These five reasons can be remembered with the acronym RIPES:

- Risk avoidance

- Image

- Productivity

- Expenses

- Security

In the final analysis, all of these are emotionally driven reasons, but productivity and expenses tend to be perceived as logically driven reasons for buying. Not surprisingly, these two reasons are often the first ones cited by buyers when we ask, "What made you decide to buy from us?" In most cases, one or more of the other three reasons for buying from you are the real reasons, and concerns about productivity and expenses are what customers use to justify their decisions to others.

Your job is to play detective and learn which motivators are in play. Our experience is that, despite what customers say initially during this interview, the strong emotional responses associated with risk avoidance are virtually always an important part of the purchase decision.

3.3.4 *Improve*

The primary Improve question is; **"How can we make it easier to become our customer?"**

This section of the Won Sales Analysis is designed to help you close more sales with those who recently experienced a *Trigger Event* by allowing you to sell more efficiently.

As we have seen, the challenge we face is that there is a

certain amount of effort required to become our customer, and a certain amount of emotional energy required to make that effort. As long as the effort required is greater than the level of emotion that buyers have around resolving the issue and solving other problems on their "to do" list, they will keep doing what they have always done. In other words, they will maintain their Status Quo and stay on the path they are on.

Trigger Events create enough emotion and motivation to make buyers get off the path they are on and start onto a new path. As you know by now, we must learn to recognize these events and act quickly on them because the emotion dissipates over time!

In the last question, we talked about the *outcome* people will get by becoming your customer. Of course, that's what your new customer will want to discuss. Now we will focus on the *process* of becoming your customer, which your new customer may not be as familiar with.

If a certain amount of effort is required to become your customer, and you find that you need to get to buyers within three weeks of experiencing a *Trigger Event* to get them to become your customer, then getting to buyers four weeks after the *Trigger Event* means that the buyer will not become your customer. Using Question #1 to learn when the events happen may help you get to motivated buyers sooner. Another way to solve this problem, however, is to diminish the amount of effort required to become your customer.

When the buyer's level of intent is higher than the perceived effort of becoming your customer, they will be in the Window of Dissatisfaction and likely to get off the path they are on and start on a new path.

You can increase the size of your potential market by diminishing the effort required to become your customer. If you can reduce the effort of becoming your customer by 50%, then you've effectively doubled the number of people who could become your customer by being able to sell to those who experienced the same *Trigger Event* up to six weeks ago!

The fact that you won the business from your new customer does not mean you have a perfect customer acquisition process. The purpose of Question #4 is to get you to focus on the hurdles related to the *process* of buying from you, not the outcome that customers actually received.

Why is this important? If you lower the hurdles that people have to overcome to become your customer, they won't have to reach as high a level of emotion to become your customer in the future. The primary hurdles are how much effort is required to find you, learn why they want to become your customer, and then buy from you.

If you don't get the kind of response you're looking for, ask a variation of the question. For instance:

- What can we do to make it easier for those looking for a solution like ours to find us?

- How can we make it easier for other people to understand the value of our solution?

- How can we make it easier for future prospects to justify buying our solution?

This question category is essential because, if people are unhappy about something related to your sales process, they generally won't complain to you about it. They will wait for somebody with a better process to show up. If, later on in the relationship, the customer has a problem and enters a Window of Dissatisfaction, you will be vulnerable.

If you have an iPhone, then answer this question: How difficult was it for you to become an iTunes customer? If you don't have an iPhone, we'll give you the answer: It's *incredibly* easy to purchase a song and download it onto your phone with iTunes.

Compare that with what happened back in the "pre-Internet" days of, the early 1990s. You were driving and heard a song on the radio, and you decided, "Hey, I'd like to play that song whenever I want to." What did you do? You had to make a note to drive to the record store—when it was convenient to do so—and buy the CD or tape you wanted.

Think of all the things that could happen before you made your purchase! Your desire to make the purchase could wane by the time you had a convenient slot open to visit the record store. Alternatively, you might have spent your money (i.e., budget) on something else or perhaps forgotten about the song entirely.

The easier you make it to become your customer, the more likely you are to get the sale!

3.3.5 *Classify*

The last section of the Won Sales Analysis allows you to classify the deals you close so that you know what to look for in the future. It also allows you to create criteria for your Trigger Event Qualifying- template discussed in Chapter 7.

Knowing what makes you win is only part of the equation. Knowing which type of deals you win is just as important. That's why the Won Sales Analysis form allows you to gather data on the type of customer you're dealing with. It helps you to understand the types of companies that are most likely to become your best customers in the future, as well as the kind of people who are most likely to experience *Trigger Events* that matter in your world.

To complete this part of the form, you must determine:

- Customer demographics
- The source of the lead
- The size of sale
- The length of the sales cycle

The customer demographics we want to focus on include the size of the business, the title and background of the decision-maker you worked with, and the type of business that became your customer. The intent is to help you identify the people you want to build a relationship with at similar companies—*before* they experience a *Trigger Event*—so that you are well-positioned to become the first person they reach out to when they do. We share a perspective on how to do this in the next chapter, which explains how to earn the status of the Emotional Favorite™.

The lead source analysis is meant to help you measure and modify your lead generation activities so as to maximize your return on lead generation activities. The idea is to determine where your best leads come from. We share some strategies for maximizing lead generation in Chapter 5, which is about Trigger Event Referrals™.

Naturally, the size of the sale is important, but not just because it determines your commission check. It's important because most organizations have a natural "sweet spot" in terms of deal size—a zone based on the monetary value of the deal where it is easiest to get sales. If you want to improve your effectiveness in identifying and winning deals that are larger than the ones you're closing now, you will find our perspective on how to do this in Chapter 6 (the Credibility Curve™).

What about the length of the sales cycle? We focus on this

aspect during this phase of the Won Sales Analysis because the shorter your sales cycle, the less likely you are to run into problems. This is similar to the prospect deciding that the time and effort of becoming your customer is too much to justify, or a new *Trigger Event* takes place in the prospect's world that makes something else a higher priority.

3.4 BENEFITS OF WON SALES ANALYSIS

The main benefit of the Won Sales Analysis is its ability to help you understand which *Trigger Events* result in the highest close ratio and the shortest sales cycle. This analysis also improves your odds of keeping the customers you've already won (and will win in the future) because it will provide you with a better sense of their expectations from the relationship.

Another key benefit of doing a Won Sales Analysis is that it allows you to gather the information necessary to qualify your opportunities effectively. For instance, once you have confirmed that the arrival of a new CFO at a target organization is one of your major *Trigger Events*, you will begin to look differently at the list of e-mail addresses that bounce back after you send out your monthly e-newsletter. One of those "dead" e-mails may serve as a flashing red light, alerting you that a CFO has left Organization A (that's one opportunity because someone has to take over the new job) and gone on to Organization B (that's another opportunity because a new CFO is coming on board).

3.5 USING THE WON SALES ANALYSIS TO CAPTURE NEW CUSTOMERS

The Won Sales Analysis is, first and foremost, an opportunity to get your *current buyers* to explain the most important *Trigger Events* to you so that you can do a better job of positioning yourself as someone *prospects* will want to talk to when those events happen.

Suppose that you find (as most salespeople do) that your most important *Trigger Event* is related to the fact that the current supplier couldn't meet a deadline, was non-responsive, or couldn't meet the buyer's requirements from a budget perspective. This fact allows you to make a powerful change in the way you communicate with your prospects. At the end of your e-mail messages, for instance, you might include a P.S. that states: "P.S.: Think of me the next time your current supplier can't meet your deadline."

You can't change the performance of the current supplier but by using this type of message, you can use what you've learned during the Won Sales Analysis to raise expectations. All things being equal, you will have a better chance of changing the prospect's perceptions and expectations if you base your communication on what you learn by completing the Won Sales Analysis.

The Won Sales Analysis will help you to track down critical information about new customer acquisition, which you might overlook during the sales process. Case in point: Tibor recently sat though presentations by three professional service firms. After all three had left, Tibor examined each sales team's leave-behinds, and noticed that one team's material was particularly colorful, powerful, and persuasive. He concluded that his own sales team could benefit by leaving behind similarly sharp-looking collateral and placed an order with a new copier supplier that a colleague had recommended for 13 heavy-duty color printers. Each cost about $5000.

To the copier salesperson, it must have seemed like manna from heaven, a miracle unlikely to be repeated—and that's the problem. He never asked what had prompted the purchase. Had the rep who received the $65,000 order practiced what we discuss in this chapter, he could have talked to every Vice President of Sales about the impact they could have on sales by allowing people to leave behind higher quality materials. Unfortunately, that rep never asked the questions we've shared with you in this chapter. We can only assume that he went back to his most familiar selling pattern. No doubt he thinks of that big sale as an anomaly. In fact, it was the key to closing more and bigger deals—faster.

SHIFT!

There are three key things to take away from this chapter:

1. THE TRIGGER EVENTS THAT BRING YOU THE BEST PROSPECTS ARE provided when you ask Questions #1 and #2 in the Won Sales Analysis.

2. WHAT GETS DECISION-MAKERS TO BECOME CUSTOMERS IS the answer you get when you ask Question #3 and shut up long enough to learn how they justified their decision to themselves and to others.

3. YOU WILL CLOSE MORE SALES BY acting on the answers to Question #4 about how we can make it easier to become our customer.

Action:

To take full advantage of what you now know, you should do the following:

1. Understand and deliver on a buyer's expectations so that you can keep them as a customer.

2. Uncover the emotional reasons people buy and what they can say to justify the decision to others.

97

3. Analyze every sale you win to better understand and start seeing more of the opportunities you are most likely to win.

Resources:

- A full sized (8.5 X 11) version and a completed example of the Won Sales Analysis template can be downloaded from www.TriggerEventBook.com/won-sales

- Special offers and information on Sales 2.0 tools and services that are related to Won Sales Analysis can be found at www.TriggerEconomy.com

CHAPTER 4

The Emotional Favorite™

"The successful man is the average man, focused."

~ Unknown

Now that you have looked inward to know who to focus on, we're going to help you look outward to see the people you want to start building relationships with.

If you don't read this chapter, you will miss out on the following:

1. Who your target customers call first when a *Trigger Event* happens

2. Who is worth taking the time and effort to build a relationship with

3. How to become the person buyers call first when a *Trigger Event* happens

4.1 BEFORE WE GET STARTED ...

Chapters 4, 5, and 6 offer concepts and strategies that work best in parallel. They do not operate in isolation, nor do they represent separate steps. They are meant to help you identify specific shifts to your selling process that you will implement over time as part of a seamless whole.

How you use the information in these chapters depends on where you are at the time, what relationship you have with a target buyer, and whether a *Trigger Event* has recently taken place. Obviously, there are several different combinations.

Knowing which combinations are in play at any given time will help you to determine which strategies and methodologies you should lead with.

Everything you learn in the second half of the book is meant to work together and support what you have learned thus far. Each of the Shifts you make in your approach as you put this program into practice will affect your overall plan for direct contact with decision-makers.

4.2 THE EMOTIONAL FAVORITE

Now that you understand how *Trigger Events* work, you are ready to learn how to get first-mover advantage when they happen. One way to get first-mover advantage is to be the first person the decision-maker calls when they decide it's time to start Searching for Alternatives. This person—called the Emotional Favorite—is the person a decision-maker knows, likes, trusts, and wants to see succeed.

People do *some* business with those they like, but they do *more* business with, and refer more business to, the person they know, like, trust, and want to see succeed—their Emotional Favorite. Consider the following story, which is based on an event that happened to one of our colleagues.

Mel works for one of the largest office supply companies in Canada. He used to start his buying discussions with purchasing agents. In prioritizing his prospecting time, he made no meaningful distinction between one purchasing agent and another. In his view, they were all equally good starting points. Unfortunately, Mel's sales cycle was long and usually difficult, and he wasn't happy with the average deal size he was securing.

One day, Mel decided to take Bill, the most successful salesperson in his organization, out for lunch and ask him some questions to determine the following:

- What did Bill do differently?

- What did Bill avoid doing altogether?

- What was Bill doing that made him such an effective salesperson?

The answers Mel heard during that hour-long lunch changed his career and his life. Bill was not targeting purchasing agents. He spent most of his prospecting time creating relationships with CFOs, and not just any CFOs: He targeted those CFOs who had just been promoted into the job or had recently been brought in from the outside.

Why the emphasis on new CFOs? Bill had conducted a Won Sales Analysis after each sale, and noticed a pattern: Companies often changed office supply vendors, or added a new office supply vendor, within 120 days of a new CFO assuming the job. The more new CFOs Bill reached out to, Mel learned, the better Bill's chances of building relationships with those who had the money and authority to do something.

Once he connected with one of these newly minted CFOs, Bill explained, he focused on becoming their Emotional Favorite, no matter what his past relationship (or lack of relationship) looked like. Bill did this work up front with as many new CFOs as possible so that he would be the one who was called when it was time for the CFO to consider new options. As a result, Bill's time to contract shrank—and his average deal size exploded!

Bill also followed CFOs who had bought from him in the past, knowing that if they bought from him before they were highly likely to buy from him again once they settled into their new jobs. He also added them to his LinkedIn network so that he always had access to their current e-mail address.

Can you guess what happened? Mel stopped calling purchasing agents, and started making friends with new CFOs!

4.3 LOGIC VERSUS EMOTION

One of the biggest mistakes that salespeople can make is believing that sales are won based upon on logic—like return on investment (ROI) calculations—rather than on emotion.

Consider all the times that you had a clear advantage in product, superior client support infrastructure, and more than competitive pricing, yet you still lost the business to someone else. Why? It didn't make sense!

Actually, it made perfect emotional sense. The buyer had a

prior relationship with their Emotional Favorite. Haven't you ever won a deal and, after signing the deal, heard the buyer tell you that, all things being equal, the other seller probably had a better offer? That offer was not "better enough" for the buyer to drop you, though. That's because you were that buyer's Emotional Favorite.

The first seller a decision-maker calls after experiencing a *Trigger Event* that starts the Searching For Alternatives process is up to five times more likely to win the business than any of the follow-on people who were contacted. That critical decision about who to call first is based upon emotion, and the first person buyers typically call is their Emotional Favorite.

Figure 4.1

In this chapter, we'll share insights and strategies on the neglected art of establishing yourself as a decision-maker's Emotional Favorite. This is an essential skill, but you should know that it is not a "quick fix" you can implement in a matter of minutes during your first conversation with everyone you talk to. To the contrary, it's a series of steps you will take over time with a carefully chosen portion of the contacts with whom you have sales discussions.

4.4 GETTING CALLED FIRST

Becoming the Emotional Favorite—the preferred person who gets called first when *Trigger Events* shift decision-makers from the Window of Dissatisfaction into Searching for Alternatives—is an art you can perfect over time, not a line you insert in your cold calling script.

There are three key reasons you want to master the art of becoming the Emotional Favorite:

1. You will get called first when a decision-maker experiences a *Trigger Event* and starts the process of Searching for Alternatives. That means you will get in front of highly motivated decision-makers before your competition.

2. By practicing the skill of searching for decision-makers who are in the Window of Dissatisfaction for things you don't sell, you will maximize the likelihood that your Selective Perception will no-

tice the Window of Dissatisfaction when decision-makers want something you do sell.

3. You will uncover opportunities for products and services you don't sell that can be passed on to people who are "In The Know" when *Trigger Events* happen to your target contact. You will learn about those In The Know and the importance of giving referrals back to those who give you referrals in the next chapter (Trigger Event Referrals).

4.5 BECOMING THE EMOTIONAL FAVORITE

To make the best use of the principles, strategies, and tactics in this chapter, you must understand three key points about becoming the Emotional Favorite, and bear them in mind as you read what follows.

4.5.1 *The Definition*

The Emotional Favorite is the person that prospective buyers typically call first when a *Trigger Event*—the event that makes them realize that it makes sense to pursue an alternate solution —starts them down the path of Searching for Alternatives.

It is essential to clearly and accurately define the Emotional

Favorite. This is not the same thing as having a good discussion with a prospect. Instead, it means being the person the prospect wants to see win and wants to use as a resource. If you've ever had a prospect call you for help with a problem that is unrelated to what you sell, you already know what it means to be the Emotional Favorite. It means that you can position yourself as the "go-to" person and maximize the likelihood of winning future business.

4.5.2 *The Actions*

People don't become the Emotional Favorite by accident. Whether they realize what they are doing or not, salespeople become the Emotional Favorites as a result of the actions they take, actions that support a certain kind of interpersonal bonding, or connection between themselves and the prospective buyer. This bonding does not happen because of a single conversation, but rather through a number of contacts, initiated by the salesperson, that play out over a series of days, weeks, or months.

4.5.3 *The Timing*

These contacts almost always happen when the prospective buyer is still in Status Quo buying mode for what you sell.

The salesperson who establishes the best relationship with the decision-maker, which aligns on shared aspirations, values, and interests while that prospective buyer is still happy with the Status Quo, can reap huge rewards. Such a salesperson will have the opportunity to be at the front of the line when the prospective buyer crosses into Searching for Alternatives mode.

That's a huge strategic and competitive advantage. If you are willing to take the steps necessary to be that first salesperson in line when the search begins (and that means, among other things, choosing your targets carefully), you can shape the buyer's perceptions of what the solution should look like. As a result, you are very likely to win not only the immediate business opportunity you are called in to discuss, but many additional opportunities that connect to other problems in that buyer's world.

4.6 PERSON TO PERSON

To become your target's Emotional Favorite, you must learn to recognize, understand, and capitalize upon the *Trigger Event* that is most likely to put that person into the Window of Dissatisfaction for things you don't sell.

This may seem like a lot of unnecessary work, but it isn't. By looking for *Trigger Events* that put decision-makers into the Window of Dissatisfaction for what you don't sell, you are finding opportunities to add value and position yourself as the Emotional Favorite and you are honing your skills to notice *Trigger Events* for the products and services you do sell.

This comes back to our message of repetition and the handwriting exercise in the introduction of this book. The more you repeat something, the easier it gets and the more likely you are to execute flawlessly when the opportunity comes up for something you sell.

As you know, a *Trigger Event* creates a change in personal priorities. We want you to start thinking of everyone within your target group who experiences an initial change in priorities as a possible "audition" for you. You are auditioning for the role of future Emotional Favorite: the person the prospective buyer knows, likes, trusts, and wants to see succeed. The person the buyer typically phones first when they start Searching for Alternatives.

In a very real sense, every business relationship is an opportunity for the parties involved to audition prospective Emotional Favorites. Just as the prospective buyer will be auditioning you, you need to evaluate whether there is a natural fit and if it is worth your time and effort to become their Emotional Favorite.

Not every buyer you talk to will be in the Window of Dissatisfaction for what you sell. Not everyone in the Window of Dissatisfaction will connect with you personally, or feel like a natural business ally. Some people, however, will feel like those kinds of instant allies. What a shame it would be to miss out on your chance for a relationship with those allies!

By the same token, no one is, or can be, everyone's Emotional Favorite. That means you should not expect to be the Emotional Favorite of every buyer you encounter. Nor should you consider a relationship that doesn't turn out to be an

Emotional Favorite situation a personal failure!

You're looking for the intersection point among three groups:

1. Those with money, authority, and influence to buy what you sell;

2. Those people with whom you have a natural chemistry, also known as psychographic fit;

3. Those people who want to see you succeed.

Only one or two of those traits is not enough. When a decision maker possesses all three traits, as shown in figure 4.2, however, you will have identified someone worth the time and effort to become the Emotional Favorite of.

Figure 4.2

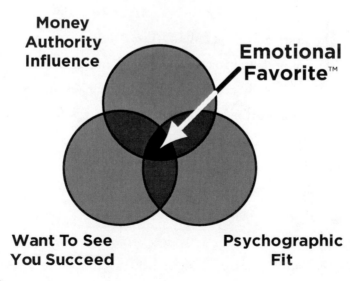

Money
Authority
Influence

Emotional
Favorite™

Want To See
You Succeed

Psychographic
Fit

4.7 THE SEQUENCE

Becoming the Emotional Favorite is a three-step process:

1. Identify those decision-makers with money, authority, and influence.

2. Decide if there is a psychographic fit.

3. Invest the time necessary to become the salesperson they want to see succeed.

4.7.1 *Money, Authority, and Influence*

Money, of course, is that chunk of the budget the decision-maker controls. Authority is formal responsibility and the ability to make a decision without having to justify it to a lot of people. Influence comes in two forms:

- Internal: The ability to influence people inside the organization to ensure the success of your solution

- External: The ability to influence decision-makers with money and influence in other organizations

You start by focusing on decision makers within your target organization (often by title, based upon your Won Sales Analysis and research) and then confirm your assumptions about money, authority, and influence through person-to-person contact.

Those you seek out must be similar to the decision-makers you identified during your Won Sales Analysis.

4.7.2 Psychographic Fit

This sounds more complicated than it actually is. A decision-maker with money, authority, and influence may not be worth your time and effort if there is no likelihood of becoming that person's Emotional Favorite, and you cannot become the Emotional Favorite of someone you have little or nothing in common with. In other words, there is little likelihood of an Emotional Favorite relationship unless both sides feel there are similarities in interests, values, or aspirations.

4.7.3 Want You to Succeed

Once you have found someone who matches the initial criteria—the kind of decision-maker you want to talk to (with money, authority, and influence) and with whom you are able to "click" on an interpersonal level—you can start building the relationship over time. The goal here is to position yourself as a long-term resource who is interested, and committed to, the goal of **helping them succeed**. You want the principle of reciprocity to kick in so that the prospective buyer starts looking for ways you can succeed, too.

4.8 EFFECTIVE TARGETING

Targeting involves asking yourself repeatedly: "Do I want to be this person's Emotional Favorite?"

Just as a "smart" missile stays on target by making changes mid-flight when it picks up a relevant change in its path toward the target, you will make correct targeting an ongoing part of your sales process. When you find yourself in a discussion with someone who does not have money, authority, and influence, you will disengage, redirect, and set a new course for the person who does.

Be proactive in helping the person you targeted. Help that person to solve problems over time, even if help takes the form of assistance and insights that are seemingly unrelated to the product or service you are trying to sell.

You will want to build the relationship over time by aligning on shared interests, values, and aspirations. Inevitably, you will find that this is far easier to do with some people than others. The more you are willing to share your interests, values, and aspiration, the more likely they are to share theirs, and the more effective you will be at making choices about whether it makes sense to invest in becoming that person's Emotional Favorite.

Of course, none of this is meant to suggest that you should stop responding to people who contact you. We do, however, want you to make a point of being proactive with those who are most likely to buy from you.

Your goal is not to help everyone for free, but rather to get a clearer sense, as time passes, of the relationships that are a priority for you. They will merit the investment of your help in the form of your unique experience, insights, and resources.

4.9 THE POWER OF TRUST

Long before the person you are targeting experiences a *Trigger Event*, you need to become trusted.

You must be trusted not just to have the decision-maker's best interests in mind, but also to deliver on what you say you will deliver. You develop this trust by becoming consistent and predictable so that the decision-maker takes on minimal risk in asking for your assistance with a problem. One way to ensure this is to be proactive by making a habit of reaching out first. This is the best way to establish predictability and reliability with the decision-maker while they are still in Status Quo mode.

Different decision-makers require different things before they trust someone enough to bestow the status of Emotional Favorite. Broadly speaking, they require evidence that the seller shares the same kinds of aspirations, values, and interests. The specific form of this evidence will vary from decision-maker to decision-maker. There is no magic formula that will work in every case.

The amount of time it will take you to create the trust to establish Emotional Favorite status will vary sharply, depending on the individual and their buying cycle. We've seen it happen in days; we've also seen it happen over a period of several months. The length of time to establish trust typically depends on the decision-maker's personality type, and the events in their past that have made them more or less risk averse. (You will learn more about the different ways buyers assess risk in Chapter 6: The Credibility Curve.)

4.10 THE POWER OF FOCUS

Do you remember the story we shared about Mel at the start of this chapter, and how he changed his focus to newly hired CFOs? A big part of the job of becoming the Emotional Favorite is narrowing your focus, and identifying a specific, narrow group of decision-makers based on your Won Sales Analysis.

We know plenty of people who knock themselves out talking to as many Boards of Directors, individual salespeople, and CEOs as possible, all in search of that elusive "golden internal referral" that will land the business and bring in a new client. The irony is that they are missing what is often the single most effective *Trigger Event* that signals the entry of the organization into the Window of Dissatisfaction: the entry of a new player at a senior level.

There's nothing wrong with internal referrals, but most of them do not and cannot effectively leverage *Trigger Events*.

Once you have completed your Won Sales Analysis and know the critical *Trigger Event* and, just as important, who it involves, you will possess a significant competitive advantage when it comes to selling. You will know exactly which people to contact and when to contact them. You will know which people within the target organization to keep on your radar screen, and you will know which people within the organization you should target to adopt you as the Emotional Favorite.

Once you learn to spot the *Trigger Event* and harness it to attain Emotional Favorite status at the right level, every other competitor will suddenly rank below you. If you make retaining and reinforcing that Emotional Favorite status a priority, then you will find that when the organization crosses over the threshold from Window of Dissatisfaction to Searching for Alternatives, you will have the inside track. You will get the first call. And you will have the chance to shape what the optimal solution looks like.

4.11 STOP SELLING ON PRICE

Remember: Becoming the Emotional Favorite is a time-consuming effort, which means that you can't expect to do it for everyone, nor must you try to do so! You must find the right point of entry.

Chad had been targeting Amalgamated Company, an industrial parts manufacturer, ever since he heard from a friend who worked there that his chief competitor's lead salesperson was moving to another state. From his Won Sales Analysis,

Chad knew that this was a *Trigger Event* likely to put decision-makers into a Window of Dissatisfaction. Chad found reasons to reach out to Brice Miller, the VP of Operations at Amalgamated Company, once a week, even though Brice made it clear that he saw no need to switch vendors, and had no intention to do so.

All the same, Chad kept finding reasons to reconnect: articles he thought Brice should see, customer referrals he might be able to use, and so on. By the fourth call, Chad had an in-depth discussion with Brice, and learned that he had a military background, as did the CEO of Amalgamated Company. Chad saw his natural opening: as it happened, he was a veteran and had served in the first Gulf War. The two spoke on the phone for nearly an hour about their shared experiences in the military.

Two weeks later, Chad got a phone call from Brice. Would he be willing to drop by and discuss some pricing and delivery questions the CEO had suddenly dropped in Brice's lap?

Within 30 days, Chad was the preferred vendor on the account.

Chad didn't try to win over and secure Emotional Favorite status with everyone in his territory or with everyone at Amalgamated Company. He focused his efforts. He targeted Brice in accordance with what he already knew about the *Trigger Event* Brice had experienced and what they had in common. In other words, he targeted Brice, and kept looking for new ways to help him and build the emerging relationship.

You might say that Chad finding out about Brice's preference for people with military backgrounds was a stroke of luck. We would reply that good salespeople make their own luck by finding as many possible points of contact with a person or an organization as possible, and then harnessing those points of contact to create Emotional Favorite status with the right person. (In Chad's case, learning about the decision-maker's military background was a piece of basic research that most of his competitors failed to perform. As it happened, the salespeople for a number of the major suppliers who worked with Amalgamated Company had some kind of military connection.)

In the end, becoming the Emotional Favorite is about auditioning for the role of problem-solver—by solving problems. Due to that, you must ask yourself three simple questions:

1. What kinds of problems does the decision-maker you have targeted face?

2. What kind of problem-solver does the decision-maker like to work with?

3. Can you be that kind of person, authentically, whether you are selling anything to this person right now or not?

The key word here is authenticity. It is authenticity within the relationship that will give you the emotional component that enables you to sell based on something other than price.

Read that again: **Emotional Favorites don't sell on price.** They don't have to discount to get the deal. Why not? Because people are willing to pay a premium for the right relationship! If you've ever lost a deal to someone whom you knew was charging a higher price than you were, you already know this much.

When you offer experience and knowledge, and nothing else, people will buy from you based on price. When your company has an established brand reputation in the marketplace, people will buy based on perceived value. That value, of course, can increase dramatically based on when you get to them (as we explained in Chapter 1).

When you start building relationships with those who have money, authority, and influence and establish yourself as the Emotional Favorite, they start making decisions based on emotion. When people buy based upon emotion, you end up with core loyal customers who are highly profitable, who are not very demanding, and who give you one of the most treasured things in sales: well-timed referrals.

4.12 NOTICING OTHER WINDOWS

How do you learn when people are in the Window of Dissatisfaction for what you don't sell so that you can harness the opportunity to become the person they want to see succeed?

If you are not learning about opportunities outside of what

is related to what you currently sell, then you are missing one of the biggest opportunities to differentiate yourself and earn Emotional Favorite status. Think about this for a moment. What would happen if you took those motivated buyers and connected them to solutions with someone from your network? You would become the "go-to person" who gets called first when there's a problem you might be able to solve. What better way to establish yourself as the Emotional Favorite?

How can you do this?

When you've finished your regular sales call, and just before you leave, you say to the buyer, "Forget what I do for ABC Company for a minute and choose one of the following:

- What's the biggest issue that you have that you just can't get to?

- What is the one thing that you're looking for that you just can't seem to find?

- What's the issue you've tried to solve but just can't find a satisfactory solution to?"

An effective way to maximize the impact of these questions, and improve the quality of the answers they yield, is to use the six second rule we shared in Chapter 3. Ask the question; listen to the answer; and wait six seconds to determine whether the person is willing to elaborate. If for some reason the silence extends for more than six seconds, calmly and tactfully repeat a few key words from the person's response. What you will find is that people will tell you about the surface problem they face, and then will drill down and tell you about the emotions behind the problem (i.e., how it impacts them and other people in the organization, and how they feel about that). Now you have enough information and knowledge to find a way to connect these motivated buyers to solutions that can help them solve that problem.

4.13 ARE YOU THE EMOTIONAL FAVORITE?

Fortunately, there is a very simple test for determining whether you are someone's Emotional Favorite. When you reach out, they typically (not always) return your call or e-mail promptly! If you are routinely ignored by the decision-maker you are targeting, you may be certain that you are *not* their Emotional Favorite yet.

Assuming that you have followed the *Trigger Event* and found someone, as Brice did, with money, authority, and influence, your challenge then becomes: How do you bring authenticity to the job you are auditioning for, which is the job of problem-solver within this new relationship you are building?

You do it by finding ways to help that don't directly connect to your product, service, or solution.

4.14 SIX RULES FOR HELPING

Becoming the Emotional Favorite is about finding the right ways to help the right people. Here are six simple rules you can follow that will make that easier.

4.14.1 *Have the Right Motive*

Your motive in offering help—whether or not it is directly related to what you are selling— must always be to make the other person look good. You're going to make that motive clear by finding a way to add value to your selling efforts, above and beyond the product or service you sell. If you're not currently selling the person anything, you're going to look for ways to make them look good to their superiors, subordinates, and peers.

Once that much is clear on both sides, your motive—supporting and building the relationship—will set you apart in the decision-maker's eyes. That will make it much easier for you to become the Emotional Favorite.

4.14.2 *Focus on the Person*

Sales is *not* about companies doing business with companies. **Sales is about people doing business with people.**

Think about this for a moment. Who is really your customer? It's not the company, but rather the person who makes the decision to buy from you. That individual is your customer. And the business that you are in—the business that we are all in—is making a specific person look good. Later on you'll get your chance to make a sale, and then you can focus on making that individual look good for choosing to buy from you rather than anybody else.

4.14.3 *Treat Them Like They Are Already Your Best Customer*

If you can find a way to make the right people look good before they buy from you, they'll make the natural assumption that they'll look a lot better once they actually buy from you.

Becoming the Emotional Favorite is about treating someone as if they are already your best customer so that they will want to become and stay one of your best customers.

A survey by Cahner's Research in 2007 showed that more than 90% of decision-makers wanted their salesperson to be more of a resource. (Not to the company, but to them as individuals!)

The people you are competing with are, in all likelihood, not following this Selling Rule. How can you take advantage of this fact? By targeting someone who matches your profile for the kind of decision-maker you want to target (who has money, influence, and authority) and who matches up well with your aspirations, values, or interests, and then treating that person as though they were already your most important customer.

4.14.4 *Keep Them Informed*

What do you do with your best customer when an opportunity arises or a problem comes up? Keep them informed, of course, and the sooner the better!

These days, people expect instant updates on what's likely to affect their world. If you plan to become the Emotional Favorite, you had better master the art of keeping your decision-maker in the loop. You must do this without being perceived as a pest (or worse, as someone who is just trying to sell something).

4.14.5 *Under-Promise and Over-Deliver*

Emotional Favorites keep their promises. If you make a commitment to a decision-maker, you must understand that that person is making commitments to other people based upon the promises you've made. If you make a commitment or promise and don't live up to it, you make them look bad. That is not in line with your intent, and it's certainly not in line with the goal of treating this person as your best customer.

When in doubt, remember the time-tested adage: under-promise and over-deliver. If you think that, if everything goes perfectly and the stars align, you can get a product, answer, or solution to your customer by Friday, make the commitment that you'll get it to them on Tuesday. They'll make commitments to other people around Tuesday. If the stars don't align, and you take until Monday to get them what you promised, that's going to make them look good to other people because you allow them to deliver early on their promises.

4.14.6 Understand Psychographics

A lot of sales "experts" will tell you that the best way to build a bond with a prospective buyer is to "match" or "mirror" that person's personality type. Sometimes this comes naturally, and if it does, that's great. There are definitely some decision-makers who will respond well to you being yourself because how you do that is in strong alignment with the way they go about being themselves. Obviously, you will want to continue your efforts to help this person and build the relationship because you and the decision-maker "click." (A fancier way of saying this is that you are in psycho-graphic alignment, but it still comes down to noticing whether you and the decision-maker "click.")

There will also be people with whom you don't click quite as easily, but you can still build a solid business relationship with them because the decision-maker values your input and is eager to take advantage of other perspectives and ways of solving problems. There is a third group of decision-makers, however, who are likely to see their own way of looking at the world (whatever that may be) as "right" and yours (if it differs) as "wrong." Steer clear of them if you can. They will inevitably make your life miserable, and their own as well.

Should you know about psychographics? Sure. Should you try to root all of your prospecting and create all of your business relationships based on your ability to memorize them, recite them, and match your own present-tense responses to buyers against them? That seems a little crazy to us.

4.15 FOUR TYPES OF PEOPLE

You may have heard about the four (or five, or nine, or sixteen) different personality types. You may have been told to memorize those specific personality types and the different ways of interacting with people who align with them. The people who told you to do this probably had the best intentions, and may have known a good deal about human psychology, but we wonder how much they know about selling.

Rather than ask you to memorize academic material you will almost certainly forget, which has never, in our experience, added much value to the effort to become an Emotional Favorite, we suggest that you consider the possibility that there are only four types of people in the world:

1. **Those who don't like you based on who they think you are.** You haven't told them who you are, and they don't know who you are. Therefore, they will make decisions based on who they think you are.

2. **Those who like you for who they think you are.**
They, too, have made assumptions about you but
don't really know you.

3. **Those who don't like you for who you really are.**
You haven't clicked because one or both of you do
not feel motivated, based on what you've learned
about each other, to invest in a professional relationship - a difference in aspirations, values, and interests.

4. **Those who like you for who you really are.** These
people know you well, know your aspirations, interests, values and interests, and want to build the
relationship. If they have money, influence, and
authority, and if they have recently experienced a
Trigger Event that puts them in the Window of
Dissatisfaction, then you want to establish Emotional Favorite status with them.

Only the last group matters!

The more people know about you, the more it will come
into the decision-making process. Yes, in some cases, when
people get to know who you really are, they may decide that
they don't like you and don't want to work with you. The real

problem here is that, if you pretend to be somebody else and win them over as a customer, at some point they will figure out who you really are, and they will leave. You will never be able to maintain Emotional Favorite status with this person. How much effort do you want to put into getting customers who aren't going to be your core, loyal customers over time?

Don't make the mistake of thinking that the key to winning Emotional Favorite status is becoming "likeable." You are not out to become likeable to every decision-maker. You want to be known as someone who excels in making carefully chosen decision-makers look good. That means entering the relationship as a peer, not a supplicant.

Establish yourself as a business equal: a problem-solver who shares interests, values, and aspirations with the decision-maker. Look for people you can establish this relationship with before the person moves into the Window of Dissatisfaction for what you sell.

Decision-makers are not looking for someone to socialize with. (That's the great flaw of the "memorize the personality type" school of sales training; they make selling sound too much like dating.) Decision-makers are looking for a shared professional outlook, a credible status as the kind of problem-solver they can work with. The conclusion you want the decision-maker to reach is "not only is this person just like me, but also when push comes to shove, I can rely on this person in battle, as this person is committed to helping me win". That's the Emotional Favorite.

4.16 PUTTING IT ALL INTO PRACTICE

We've shared some strategies that you can use to start this relationship building process and get you closer to becoming the Emotional Favorite. Now it's time for you to use those strategies.

There are many ways to put these ideas into action. For instance, start asking your customers to share the names of suppliers who are already their Emotional Favorites. Use these discussions to create a pool of people you can use to pass on referrals to people when you hear that they're looking for something you don't sell. Then you can say, "You know what, I had a customer with a similar need, and here's who they used." Not only will you strengthen your relationship with the person, you will also improve your relationships with the suppliers, who will appreciate the leads you send their way and will find a way to reciprocate. You might want to consider drafting an e-mail that asks your customers for this information. Once you send it out, you'll find that some of your current customers will reach out to you more often for help and advice and start sending more business your way.

You can also use social media tools like LinkedIn, Facebook, or Twitter to implement the ideas you've learned here. These tools can definitely make the process of becoming the Emotional Favorite simpler.

SHIFT!

There are three key things to take away from this chapter:

1. THE FIRST PERSON A DECISION MAKER CALLS when a *Trigger Event* makes them want something is their Emotional Favorite.

2. THOSE WORTH BUILDING A PROACTIVE RELATIONSHIP WITH are decision-makers, similar to the ones identified in your Won Sales Analysis, that have money, authority, and influence, and share your aspirations, values, and interests.

3. YOU BECOME THE FIRST PERSON DECISION MAKERS CALL by aligning your motives and aspirations to theirs.

Action

To take advantage of what you now know, you should do the following:

1. Stop trying to be liked by everyone and start being loved by those who matter the most.

2. Differentiate yourself from your competitors by always asking decision-makers about problems that are not related to what you sell.

3. Build an Emotional Favorite relationship strategy based on the Emotional Favorite worksheet so that you can start building relationships with those who are highly likely to become influential decision-makers in the future, not just those who have that status today.

Resources

- A full sized (8.5 X 11) version and a completed example of Emotional Favorite strategy worksheet can be downloaded from www.TriggerEventBook.com/emotional-favorite

- Special offers and information on Sales 2.0 tools and services that are related to becoming the Emotional Favorite, such as LinkedIn , can be found at www.TriggerEconomy.com

CHAPTER 5

Trigger Event Referrals™

The tip of the iceberg is just a spec of what lies below the waterline
~ ISSAC NEWTON

You might be getting a few referrals for visible opportunities that are above the water today, but odds are you are missing out on a significant number of visible opportunities that are below the water.

If you don't read this chapter, you will miss out on the following:

1. How to get better referrals from your existing network of contacts

2. Who is "In The Know" when decision-maker's experience a *Trigger Event* and suddenly want what you sell

3. How to get those "In The Know" to introduce you to decision-makers at EXACLTY the right time

---

In the 1980s, Craig got his first sales job working for a company called AMP of Canada. He was hired as a telemarketer to handle all accounts in Western Canada that had sales of less than $10,000.

Back then, AMP had three distributors in his territory: Hamilton Hallmark, ITT, and Cardinal. He wanted to grow his territory so that he could be promoted to outside sales. He started building relationships with inside and outside salespeople with the distributors who were selling the most in his top accounts. He then developed sales opportunities within his accounts and then passed those opportunities onto the salespeople for the distributors.

Craig was applying the Emotional Favorite strategy you learned in Chapter 4 to those who were often "In the Know" before he was. It did not take long for these distributor salespeople to recognize the value of the opportunities they were being given and soon they started reciprocating by bringing him in on opportunities that they had discovered.

Can you guess what happened? Just 90 days after he joined AMP as a telemarketer, he was promoted to outside sales. He kept his focus on building relationships with and adding value to those "In the Know" about opportunities before him. As a result, he was promoted and transferred twice in the next three years and selected for AMP's "Captain's Club" for distinguished sales excellence.

If you are looking to increase sales in the territory you already have and earn the opportunity to take over a more senior territory, read on to learn more about how to get those "In the Know" to introduce you to decision-makers after they experience a *Trigger Event* but before they have found the time to call their Emotional Favorite.

5.1 WHAT ARE YOU DOING NOW?

Think of the total number of referrals you could generate over the next 12 months. We could picture those referrals as an iceberg.

You may already be getting the occasional referral from a customer or acquaintance, but we're willing to bet that the referral was about an opportunity that is above the surface. In other words, it's active and open for your competition to also see.

You will probably miss 90% of the referrals you could get over the next 12 months because you are not connected to people who know most of the relevant opportunities that will surface during the next year. Most salespeople have not mastered the art of pro-actively generating referrals that will most likely turn into business. In this chapter, we show you how to master that art.

Very often, salespeople are told to "generate referrals" by asking current customers and/or their best prospects for the names of other decision-makers. They are told to say, in so many words, "Who else should I contact that would benefit from working with ABC Company?" Then they're told to exercise the willpower necessary to wait out the (inevitable) awkward silence that follows.

What happens after that long pause? Well, in most cases, the customer or prospect tells you that no one comes to mind. (By the way, that's usually true. People generally don't think well when they're put on the spot and you've just put your customer on the spot.)

Sometimes, though, you get a response that sounds something like, "Hmmm. You know who you might want to talk to? Jim Smith over at Consolidated Company. I remember that he had a big widget program going a while back. You could give him a call."

Following the instructions you received, you get Jim's contact information, and confirm with your contact that it is "alright to use your name" when reaching out to Jim. For a moment, you think that you've reached the Promised Land.

When you finally connect with Jim, what happens? Our bet is that you almost always find that Jim is in Status Quo mode. In other words, you may have just met someone interesting, but the timing wasn't quite right. Jim does not yet see a reason to change the Status Quo, and this is (you now know) not the ideal time to connect with Jim if you want to make a sale in the short term. The few times that Jim is not in Status Quo, odds are he has already started the process of Searching for Alternatives and has a preferred supplier.

You come away from your discussion with Jim disappointed.

5.2 TWO FUNDAMENTAL FLAWS

Between us we have worked with thousands or salespeople and business owners over the years. Most of them admit that they are not as effective in soliciting quality referrals as they would like to be. We see two fundamental flaws when it comes to the process people typically use to generate referrals.

Flaw #1: Timing

To begin, they are getting referred to those who are either in buying modes of Status Quo or Searching for Alternatives.

Flaw #2: Referral Target

People are asking for referrals to the wrong people. Rather than seek referrals direct to buyers, they should seek referrals to People In The Know about *Trigger Events* and the decisions or purchases that precede them. These, of course, are the same *Trigger Events* you identified in your Won Sales Analysis.

Most salespeople request referrals in a way that is almost certain to keep them from finding and closing a short-term opportunity. Two critical questions that usually go unasked are:

1. What kind of referrals should I be asking for?

2. Who should I be targeting to improve my timing?

Unless you choose the right target, the referrals you receive are unlikely to result in revenue in either the short or medium term. You may repeat the familiar process a few times because you know that you are supposed to ask for referrals. However, because of the two flaws in the process, it will continue to be ineffective. As a result, you will either consciously or unconsciously conclude that the business of asking for referrals is a complete waste of time.

It is a waste of time... if you insist on trying to generate referrals in the way that most of you have been trained to do.

5.3 THE WRONG WAY TO GET REFERRALS

Let's look more closely at the way that most salespeople are trained to ask for referrals by sales managers, trainers, or others who don't have personal responsibility for generating revenue. If you've read this far, we think that you'll quickly spot the problem. Once you spot it, you'll understand why so many salespeople find many reasons to avoid this essential part of the sales process.

A large percentage of salespeople we've worked with or trained haven't made any attempt to generate referrals in a long time. They prefer to rely on the natural referrals that arise. How do these referrals arise? They materialize when someone In the Know reaches out to the salesperson with information about an emerging opportunity.

In the best cases, these People In the Know point you toward buyers who have just experienced *Trigger Events*, and have not yet called an Emotional Favorite. But do sales managers and sales trainers typically tell you to target those People In the Know as your first referral priority? If you are like most salespeople, the answer is no.

So what are they trying to get you to do? Waste your time! They may not realize it, of course, but that's what they're doing; if you can get one of them to read this chapter, they'll understand why they're wasting your time. Nine times out of ten, when you follow their instructions to generate a referral from a current customer or prospect, the person you end up talking to is either:

- In Status Quo mode (where there is an entrenched competitor, in which case you wonder why your contact gave you the name in the first place);

or

- In Searching for Alternatives mode (where there is a preferred solution and a preferred supplier, probably one who enjoys Emotional Favorite status).

In both scenarios, the result is the same to your bottom line: You're out of the running. No wonder you stopped having this kind of conversation with your customers!

Now that you've read Chapter 4, you have a method for deciding whether the person you are referred to while they are in Status Quo mode is worth spending time with. You also have a strategy for becoming the person they phone first when they experience a *Trigger Event* in the future. Now it's time to take this to the next level. You want to get referrals to decision makers who will buy from you in the near future.

What can you do differently to make that a reality?

5.4 GETTING THE BEST REFERRALS

What if you made a commitment, beginning today, to create more relationships with the right people—the People In the Know—who are positioned to notice (and tell you about) the events, decisions, and purchases that are most likely to precede the *Trigger Events* you identified in your Won Sales Analysis?

What if you made a point of taking action to follow through on that commitment by shifting your strategy at networking events?

What if you conducted a self-check at least once a month to see how well you were doing in the area of measurably expanding your personal base of People In the Know?

If you made this commitment, you would be on your way to finding and implementing a way to secure many more of the best referrals. You would be seeing a bigger chunk of the iceberg instead of just the tip.

The way to get better referrals is to get referred to the decision-maker immediately after they have experienced the *Trigger Event* that puts them in the Window of Dissatisfaction, but before they start investigating options or call their Emotional Favorite.

As figure 5.1 below illustration suggests, the best way to improve the quality of your referrals is to improve the quality of your timing. You can start doing that right now. To improve your timing, however, you will need to start targeting someone other than the decision-maker.

Figure 5.1

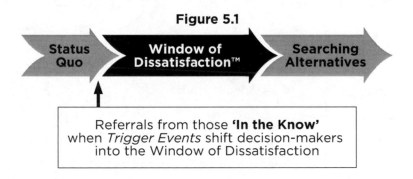

that puts them in the Window of Dissatisfaction

When it comes to referrals, you will need to stop focusing on customers as your primary referral source. Instead, you must start identifying, and creating relationships with, People In the Know about the events, decisions, and purchases that lead up to the decision-maker buying what you sell

5.5 A BETTER REFERRAL SOURCE

Getting People In the Know to notice, and forward, Trigger Event Referrals to you whenever they become known is easier than you may think it is. The first essential step involves changing your assumptions. You must begin by accepting that there are people who know about a lot more opportunities than your customers do.

Most of your customers are too busy putting out fires in their world to notice changes outside that world that may affect you. This is the main reason you often hear that awkward pause when you ask for names of people you can call. Rather than ask, "How do I get more referrals from my customers?" you should be asking, "Where am I getting my highest quality referrals from right now, and how do I maximize that process?" This is an important change in intent, and it is the foundation of everything you will learn in this chapter.

If you think about the natural referrals you have received in the past year—those times when someone on your Rolodex who wasn't a customer reached out and dropped an opportunity in your lap that led to business—you'll get a clearer sense of the process you should be trying to replicate. You could think of this as a form of Won Sale Analysis: One that is focused on the source of the sale rather than the sale itself.

What happened when you received that referral? Your contact, whoever it was, came across a valuable piece of information about a critical event, decision, or purchase that resulted in a specific decision-maker experiencing a *Trigger Event* that pushed them into the Window of Dissatisfaction. That single event, decision, or purchase had the potential of connecting to your product or service. And your contact noticed it and called you about it before calling anyone else.

In other words, your contact was suddenly In the Know about something that could affect you, and decided to bring you into the loop. The Person In the Know chose to share knowledge and insights with you about what was happening on the ground, and what might happen next, in a given decision-maker's world. As a result, you got in the door after the *Trigger Event* and before the decision-maker selected a solution type or preferred supplier.

Why did it happen? There are a variety of possible explanations, all of which are worth understanding. Maybe you got that referral because your contact was thanking you for the referrals you generated for them in the past (a principle we all know as reciprocation). Or perhaps your contact wanted to become the buyer's Emotional Favorite, and knew that referring you would help the buyer look good in the eyes of superiors or subordinates. Maybe your contact realized that working together as a team was better than going it alone. Perhaps you showed the Person In the Know how to provide a whole solution rather than a partial solution, and that offering made it easier for someone to buy from your contact. Whatever you did, you earned the treasured Emotional Favorite status of the Person In the Know and became the person they refer at exactly the right time.

Almost without meaning to, you were each on the lookout for new ways to help each other. This raises the question:

What would happen if you did this on purpose?

5.6 HOW MANY PEOPLE "IN THE KNOW" ARE ON YOUR RADAR SCREEN?

Seemingly out of the blue, an old acquaintance phoned Bill and asked whether he was still doing consulting work in the field of social media marketing. Bill assured his friend Sally, an executive recruiter, that he was still active in that area. "I have someone I think you should call," said Sally. "He's just been named Vice President of Marketing at Big Co, and he's supposed to put together a social media program ASAP. His name is Wendell Martin. Can you give him a call?"

When it comes to getting referrals that reflect *Trigger Events*, you have to remind yourself of something very, very important: **The more "Sallys" you have on your radar screen, the more "Wendells" you will be in a position to call!**

Consider this true story. Tibor was recently working with a Vice President of Sales at a large imaging company. After a few months of working on basic skills training, it became apparent that the company needed to get its managers focused on better managing and coaching around the company's sales process. The VP was keen on this idea and, more importantly, had a budget with which to execute it. From experience, Tibor knew that it would be difficult for the front line to adhere to the process and for the managers to have the visibility to help their teams by coaching without a Customer Relationship Management (CRM) program. The VP acknowledged that the company had known it needed a CRM for some time, but had failed to take action. He did see the upside of having a CRM process in place and believed the lack of a process was holding back both the team and company.

As a result, Tibor called Saul, a rep with a leading CRM provider, with whom he had worked in the past; a number of Tibor's clients had implemented Saul's CRM program. (Interestingly enough, Saul practiced the referral development practices we are sharing with you in this chapter. Tibor had initially come to know Saul because Saul had targeted him for referral swaps at several sales-related events.

Tibor told Saul about his conversation with the VP, and the fact that a number of the objectives the VP was looking to achieve were connected to the sales process. That sales process would require a CRM program. Saul called the VP, who was happy to hear from Saul--based on Tibor's introduction at exactly the right time. Saul got the business.

So, ask yourself these four questions:

1. How many People In the Know are on your radar screen?

2. How many People In the Know have you on their radar screen?

3. How many People In the Know are aware of the profiles for people and *Trigger Events* you uncovered in your Won Sales Analysis?

4. How many People In the Know have you talked to about the events, decisions, and purchases that lead up to the *Trigger Events* that create demand for what you sell?

5.7 THE THREE CS

Most of you can think of at least one relationship you have, right now, with a Person In the Know—a person who has given you invaluable intelligence about decision-makers who have experienced the events, decisions, and purchases that connect to the *Trigger Events* you're on the lookout for. The challenge is that, all too often, you've simply stumbled into these precious In the Know relationships. They may seem to have happened by accident! Yet these accidents are worth finding a way to repeat because our experience is that a Person In the Know can deliver eight to ten times more referrals than a customer. You read that right: **eight to ten times more referrals!**

Most salespeople do not have enough active relationships with People In the Know!

There are three different kinds of People In the Know for you to reach out to, each requiring a different approach. They're called **Complementors, Competition, and Connections.**

5.7.1 *Complementors*

As the name suggests, Complementors sell a complementary product or service to what you sell. This group is incredibly important in terms of delivering Trigger Event Referrals because one purchase decision often leads to a situation that connects directly to a different, but complementary, purchase decision.

For those who sell life insurance, the primary *Trigger Event* that results in couples finally getting life insurance is the birth of their first child. So, what kind of person would be a perfect Complementor for someone who sells life insurance? It might be a real estate agent or mortgage broker. Those people talk to couples every day who are about to have (or are thinking of having) their first child, and who are looking for a first home they can move into now. They do it now because they don't want to be moving near the date the baby is scheduled to arrive.

If you had to choose between getting referrals to a dozen couples who may or may not have recently experienced a

Trigger Event and getting referrals from a dozen real estate agents who sell homes to young couples who recently moved into their first home, which group would you choose?

Consider Harvey, who sells cabling and racks for installations of servers and other computer equipment. One of his Complementors is Jack, who helps companies to design and relocate data centers. Harvey is also a Complementor for Steve, who sells cooling systems for equipment rooms.

5.7.2 Competition

Competition refers to alternate solutions that someone may buy to get the same outcome that you provide. Remember that it's not the same thing as your competitors, who are an alternative provider of the same or similar solution.

For example, we sell sales training. Our competitor also sells sales training, and that person is probably not going to be a good source of Trigger Event Referrals for us. But your Competition is not the same as your competitor. The Competition is someone who sells a *different* product or service that is perceived as providing the same outcome that someone would get from working with us. This could be someone who sells software that improves sales efficiency, or it could be a marketing consultant, a strategy consultant, or a business coach. Your Competition doesn't compete with you in terms of the category of the *stuff* you sell, as a competitor would. However, the Competition competes with you for a share of the same *budget line*.

Obviously, you won't get very far if you plan to get Trigger Event Referrals from competitors who are trying to sell the same product, service, or solution to the same universe of target buyers. On the other hand, if you are willing to reach out to people who provide alternate solutions to problems similar to the ones you solve, you are likely to find some who are In the Know, who occasionally compete for the same budget line, and who are willing to put you on their radar screen (and are eager to get onto yours). These people are your Competition, not your competitors, and they can be excellent sources of information about what is happening to launch *Trigger Events*—and new revenue opportunities—that you can capitalize on.

Why will the Competition give you referrals? There are the two main reasons:

1. They know that recommending complementary providers like you demonstrates to the customer they care about making them successful and this maximize the likelihood they will get new referrals from that customer

2. They know you will reciprocated by giving them referrals back

In our field, the Competition would be people and companies that conduct appraisals of salespeople. They compete for the same budget line that we do, but they do not sell the same service. You can and do co-exist, and add value for a lot of different buyers. Another example might be a company that sets appointments for B2B sales forces. While such companies may be good at getting these appointments, the ultimate measure of success is the actual improvement in revenues and clients closed.

With that in mind, it is worthwhile for us to reach out to these companies because it is in their interest to make sure that the appointments they set are maximized by a better trained and capable sales force. The fact that we occasionally compete for the same budget line is almost incidental, just as it is in the case of the company that conducts personnel assessments of sales staffs. We are excellent referral sources for each other.

5.7.3 Connections

The Connection is anyone else who has regular access to, and sells to, the people you want to turn into customers.

Some people hear us talking about Connections during our programs and assume that we are talking about "networking." That's partially true. What most people mean by networking is handing out your business card to everyone you can, collecting as many business cards as you can, and then calling everyone back (or at least attempting to do so). With this kind of networking, there's no real purpose, no system in place for prioritizing who is most important to follow up with, and no target.

When we talk about identifying Connections, we are talking about noticing, and reaching out to, a specific group of people: those who sell products and services that decision-makers who experience a *Trigger Event* have bought or are going to buy. These purchases may not lead directly to an event that reminds the buyer about the importance of making a decision to buy what you sell, as they would in the case of the Complementor. (Consider: The real estate agent closes the home sale with the couple who is about to have a baby and, all of a sudden, the issue of buying life insurance seems more important.)

Even so, knowing what Connections sell, and when and how, helps you to identify more people who are likely to have experienced the *Trigger Event* you identified in your Won Sales Analysis. Think of Connections as the answer to this question: "What else do decision-makers who are still in the Window of Dissatisfaction need?" or "Who else has customers that I want as customers?"

As sales training professionals, some of your ideal Connections are accountants. Why? Because they know when there is a change in business ownership or ownership structure. This is one event that leads up to people deciding they want to grow their business and start thinking about (you guessed it) sales training.

For example, if you sell network or telephony systems and services, then you know that an organization's moves, changes, or additions almost always lead to a need for your services. Knowing that, you want to have as many relationships as possible with those who sell to the same decision-makers you want to access—and thus learn of these moves, changes, or additions before your competition does. In this case, having a relationship with office furniture suppliers, printing companies, and Web developers would be of interest. All of these people will hear about moves, product/service changes, or personnel additions before you will. They will hear about the events, decisions, and purchases that affect you, and be in a position to tell you about them while the decision-maker is still in the Window of Dissatisfaction, giving you a head start on your competition. Obviously, you want to make friends with these people and, if possible, hand them referrals!

5.8 GETTING MORE REFERRALS FROM BETTER REFERRAL SOURCES

The referrals you receive from customers still have value, of course, and we're not trying to minimize their value. Our goal is to give you the tools that will help you to connect, and create lasting relationships, with more In the Know contacts who can send you multiple high-value referrals. They are the ones that will tell you about the critical events, decisions, and purchases that will help you to reach decision-makers who have just entered, or are about to enter, the Window of Dissatisfaction.

Once you have identified People In the Know, you must earn the privilege of getting timely Trigger Event Referrals from them. Start feeding these people good prospects and watch the quality referrals come your way.

A survey of more than 200 sales managers and salespeople yielded the following intriguing results:

- Salespeople reported that they learned of additional customer needs (i.e., opportunities for someone else to sell something that they did not sell) approximately 3.14 times a month, or almost 38 times a year.

- The average value of each opportunity was greater than $25,000.

- Salespeople reported giving one-third of these referrals to a company that partnered with their employer, and another one-third to someone they knew. They simply ignored the remaining one-third because they had no one to pass them to.

We suspect the one-third of referrals given to people they know could be redirected to you because, most of the time, the person receiving the referrals does not do a solid job of recognizing (saying, "Thank You") or reciprocating.

5.8.1 Focus, Focus, Focus

When it comes to referral relationships, you don't want to try connecting with everyone. Instead, target your efforts. Pick a specific geographical region (e.g., greater Calgary) and start there in your search for Complementors, Competition, and Connections who will put you on their referral radar screen. Then, within the region you select, identify a few industries where you have expertise, insights, and existing relationships.

Can you move beyond the city and industries you've selected if a Person In the Know points you in an interesting direction? Of course! But by starting within a relatively small base of organizations in a certain region, you're increasing the likelihood that a certain group of People In the Know, who talk to each other on a regular basis, will hear your name more than once. That makes it much easier to build new relationships. As Will Rogers once put it, "When you get someone else to blow your horn, the sound will travel twice as far."

5.8.2 *Become Their Emotional Favorite*

Almost everything you learned in Chapter 4 about securing the Emotional Favorite status with decision-makers is applicable to your efforts to create the same kind of relationship with Complementors, Competition, and Connections.

Keep an eye out for the interests of every Person In the Know for whom you want to be the Emotional Favorite. Bear in mind that winning Emotional Favorite status with People In the Know (or anyone else) is not a matter of "who you know," nor is it a matter of "who knows you." Instead, it's a matter of who knows you, likes you, trusts you, and wants you to succeed.

5.8.3 *Always Have a Target*

When you go to a conference, trade show, or networking event, go with the intent of being introduced to People In the Know. Make it a point to ask everyone you can about what they do, who they came with, and how they know the event host or sponsor. You're not just being sociable, although being sociable is wonderful. You're extending your Trigger Event Referral antennae for People In the Know who are at the event. You want to know:

- How many potential Complementors showed up tonight?

- How many approachable representatives of the Competition are here?

- How many Connections did I just see by the punch bowl?

- How could I meet these people and start building a mutually rewarding relationship?

You certainly won't ignore targeted decision-makers who happen to be in attendance at the event. In most cases, though, you will encounter more People In the Know than prospective decision-makers who can buy what you sell. Make the most of the opportunity; take advantage of the face time.

5.8.4 *The Seven Second Sale*

Many of you have been told to prepare and practice a "30-second elevator pitch" so that you have an answer when someone asks, "What do you do?"

The 30-second pitch may have its applications (such as at the beginning of a formal presentation) but it is fatally flawed in networking settings. Thirty seconds is far too much conversational real estate to seize at the beginning of a conversation with a new acquaintance. If you doubt this, think of the last time you were bored by someone who went on and on about how great their product was and why everyone you know would want to become their customer.

At most events, you have about seven seconds to work with. If your message lasts longer than that, you can assume that the person you've met has already forgotten the first words you said. Their eyes will glaze over, and they'll start looking around the room for people they would rather talk to. Instead of a 30-second elevator pitch, think in terms of a Seven Second Sale—an intriguing conversation starter that gives the other person a chance to participate in a dialogue with you. When they ask you what you do, tell them who you help and the outcome they get from being your customer in seven seconds or less!

Here's what our Seven Second Sale sounds like:

New acquaintance: "So, Craig, what do you do?"

Craig: "We help salespeople sell more by changing what they see."

New acquaintance: "How do you do that?" or "What do you mean by that?"

Either of these highly desirable responses—or virtually any other response—achieves the objective, which is to begin a back-And-forth exchange about what we do. That's more effective than beginning the conversation with a lecture about what we do!

With the Seven Second Sale, you're declining the opportunity to deliver a monologue the other person will inevitably ignore or forget. Instead, you're using your precious opening seconds in the encounter to connect on a personal or business level. Now the Person In the Know you're talking to is actually curious. You've begun a conversation; in our case, we can share a few things related to timing, *Trigger Events*, and getting to people early. One of the most satisfying moments comes when a Person In the Know, who was initially resistant to the idea of selling more by changing what you see, eventually says, "You know what? Now that you mention it, I can see what triggered some of my big wins in the past. Now I'll be looking for those events so I can replicate those big wins."

5.8.5 *Don't Sell, Don't Sell, Don't Sell!*

This may be the most difficult piece of advice in the entire book. You must resist the opportunity to sell during networking events. Everyone else will be selling. You will ask good questions. You will not pitch your products or services. You will not ask for the names of possible buyers of your product or service. You will not ask the Person In the Know to think of you first and call you when they run into a decision-maker.

Instead, you will ask a question sequence that covers the following broad topic areas:

- **What does this person do for a living?** This is the most important question from a strategic point of view. Once you have connected with a Person In the Know—a Complementor, some part of the Competition you can work with, or a Connection— you will keep looking for reasons to prolong the conversation. Of course, you will also keep looking for reasons to keep talking if you happen to run into a potential decision-maker. With anyone else, you will politely and tactfully look for the nearest conversational off-ramp.

- **How did this person get into the business?** Notice that you are focusing on workplace and business issues. Your goal is not to learn about what is and isn't working in this person's family life. If the conversation goes off track, gently redirect it to the business issues you want to learn about. In most cases, you will find that people are more than happy to share their career history. If you listen closely, you can learn of the *Trigger Events* that caused someone to switch jobs. You can harness this information knowing that people you want to sell to could experience something similar.

- **What significant changes has this person seen in their industry?** What are the coming trends? With these questions, you're giving the other person a chance to share insights, experiences, and predictions. Again, listen closely because there may be some *Trigger Events* you can harness in your own territory. For us, the last and most important question always sounds like this:

- **If I could use my connections or network to assist you in any way, what way would that be?** Think about that question for a moment. It is about as far as you can get from what generally happens when salespeople sell at these events by asking the person to share the names of decision-makers. Yet our experience has shown, time and time again, that it is the most powerful question when it comes to building relationships that deliver referrals to people in the Window of Dissatisfaction. When you ask a Person In the Know how you can put your network to work for their business, you open the floodgates. The person you're talking to will go into detail about the specific profiles they are looking for in terms of ideal customers, employees, or business partners. At the end of that discussion, you will often hear something like, "Thanks for offering to help out. How can I return the favor?"

This moment, to paraphrase Humphrey Bogart in "Casablanca," is the beginning of a beautiful friendship. The problem is most people miss the opportunity by saying something like "don't worry about it, I'll call you if I think of something in the future."

When you get a detailed response to this question, don't say "don't worry about it" or ask for a referral to a target decision-maker. Instead, ask for a referral to someone else who is In the Know. You might say, "I would love an introduction to an accountant or a marketing consultant so that we can work together for mutual benefit." (Of course, you would replace "accountant" or "marketing consultant" with a Person In the Know, and then ask them about what leads up to the *Trigger Events* that connect to your product or service.)

By asking this question, you make it clear that your motive is not just to sell something, but to make the person you're working with, whoever it may be, successful. Believe it: This question increases the likelihood that the person you're talking to will eventually either point you toward a decision-maker who has recently experienced a *Trigger Event* that matches with your area of specialty or (just as valuable) point you toward another Person In the Know.

It is a virtual certainty that the person you are talking to will ask for more information about what a good business opportunity looks like to you. Use this discussion to describe the *Trigger Event* that puts your ideal prospect into the Window of Dissatisfaction.

5.8.6 *Follow those "In the Know"*

Relationships with People In the Know are precious. They do not always yield immediate dividends. They must be nurtured over time, and that often means following the Person In the Know from one job to another.

In today's fast-moving world, it is inevitable that a Person In The Know with whom you have laid the foundations for a mutually beneficial business relationship will move on, perhaps to a new job, a new company, or a new industry. Follow this person to their next career destination, and stay in touch!

By doing so, you will have the potential to identify as many as three important new opportunities to expand your valuable personal network of People In the Know:

1. The new organization your Person In the Know now works for;

2. The person who took over your Person In the Know's old job.(we'll call them Person In the Know B);

3. The person who took over Person In the Know B's old job, wherever that was.

Use business networking sites such as LinkedIn to keep in touch with and keep track of job changes among your network of People In the Know. Use these sites to follow the comings and goings of decision-makers because the same multiple-opportunity dynamic arises when they change jobs:

1. Those who purchased from you in the past are highly likely to buy from you again in their new role.

2. Those who take the place of the person you used to sell to could give you a greater share of their purchases.

3. The person who took the place of your initial contact is new in their job and now is the time they are more likely time to become your customer.

SHIFT!

There are three key things to take away from this chapter:

1. TO GET BETTER REFERRALS YOU NEED TO ask for introductions to those who have either just experienced or are about to experience a *Trigger Event* that results in decision-makers buying from you.

2. PEOPLE IN THE KNOW ARE Complementors, Competition, and Connections who have as customers those you want as customers.

3. YOU WILL GET MORE REFERRALS WHEN you become the Emotional Favorite of people "In the Know" when a decision-maker experiences a *Trigger Event*.

Action

To take advantage of what you now know, you should do the following:

1. Tell your referral sources that you are looking for decision-makers who have experienced the specific *Trigger Events* that bring you business.

2. Look for and get introduced to People In the Know when you go to networking events.

3. Analyze every sale you win to better understand who are your best referral sources.

Resources

- A full sized (8.5 X 11) version and a completed example of the Trigger Event Referrals worksheet can be downloaded from www.TriggerEventBook.com/trigger-event-referrals

- Special offers and information on Sales 2.0 tools and services that are related to Trigger Event Referrals can be found at www.TriggerEconomy.com

CHAPTER 6

The Credibility Curve™

*The toughest thing about the power of trust is that it's very difficult
to build and very easy to destroy."*

~ Thomas J. Watson

Even if you get in front of highly motivated decision makers at exactly the right time you are unlikely to win the sale if you don't minimize the perception of the risk they take on by becoming your customer.

Getting in front of highly motivated decision-makers at exactly the right time will help to put solid opportunities into your sales funnel. However, there are still two things you need to do to maximize the likelihood you will close those opportunities:

1. Make it less risky to be your customer (covered in this chapter).

2. Make the most of your first call or visit (covered in Chapter 7).

If you don't read this chapter you will miss out on the following:

1. Understanding the biggest killer of sales - risk

2. Learning how to diminish the two components of risk

3. Discovering the three types of credibility that overcome a buyer's perception of risk

6.1 OVERCOMING RISK

Here's the bottom line. When decision-makers who have experienced a *Trigger Event* don't buy from you, the most common reason is simple: They perceived the risk of becoming your customer as being too high! Will they say as much to your face? Probably not. But when you encounter multiple so-called objections in the sales effort (e.g., the timing isn't right, the budget authority is not in place, the data you offered is insufficient), the underlying cause of the deal not closing is often the decision-maker's perception of an unacceptable level of risk of doing business with you.

It amazes us that most salespeople spend little or no time consciously dealing with the buyer's adversity to risk. In our experience, the biggest killer of sales is risk.

The decision-maker perceives the risk of being your customer to be too high.

To overcome this risk, you need to develop credibility.

Your first challenge is the instant you start trying to sell to a prospect they start thinking about all the risks of buying from you, as shown on the left of figure 6.1.. The best way to offset risk is with credibility, also shown in figure 6.1.

Your second challenge is that credibility takes time to build, shown in figure 6.1 below.

Figure 6.1

Your third challenge is that time is short when you are try-ing to capitalize on the emotion and related intention of buy-ing, which is created by *Trigger Events*, as shown in figure 6.2 below.

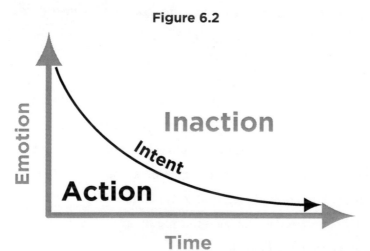

Figure 6.2

6.2 CAN I WIN THE SALE YET?

Let's look at how risk plays out in the world of selling.

In figure 6.1, the time since the buyer's experience of a *Trigger Event* is measured from left to right. The professional seller's perceived credibility begins low on the scale, but moves up over time as the relationship deepens. When you are above the Credibility Curve, the decision-maker perceives you as presenting more risk than credibility. Above the Credibility Curve, your odds of getting the sale—even when you have first-mover advantage—are low.

On the other hand, if you are on or below the Credibility Curve, you are perceived as presenting less risk than credibility. In this situation, your odds of getting the sale by harnessing *Trigger Events* to create first-mover advantage are high.

A Credibility Curve that seems too lengthy (from our point of view) is not the only dynamic in play. What is also in play is the buyer's Curve of Diminishing Intent, which we discussed earlier. The combination of these two is shown in figure 6.3, with the lightly shaded area representing where you have credibility while the buyer still intends to do something about moving from their current solution.

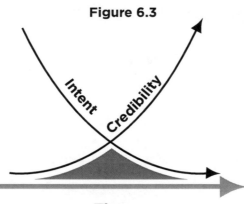

Figure 6.3

Time

6.3 THE WINDOW OF DISSATISFACTION

Let's look at the third factor: the decision-maker's level of dissatisfaction with the current solution (also known as the Status Quo).

Figure 6.4

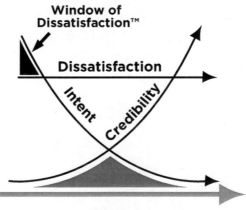

Time

Notice the dark triangle in the top left corner of figure 6.4. It represents the Window of Dissatisfaction. This is where the buyer's intent overlaps the buyer's dissatisfaction. This is exactly where you want to be to maximize the likelihood that you will harness the *Trigger Event* that led to the Window of Dissatisfaction.

The area above the dark line (in figure 6.4) describes buyers who are dissatisfied with the performance of the solution they are currently using; they are highly likely to switch suppliers. Below the dark line, the buyer is satisfied with what they have, which means that it's easier to maintain the Status Quo than it is to buy from you

In figure 6.4, the Window of Dissatisfaction is represented by the shaded area above the horizontal line that represents their level of dissatisfaction and below the line that represents their diminishing intent.

The lightly shaded area, where buyer still have intention and you have credibility, reflects the time that decision-makers will consider buying from you. As you can see, if we let things run their course and build the relationship over time, the likelihood of closing the sale is pretty much zero.

If the lightly shaded area was above the dark line, the buyer would be dissatisfied enough to invest some time to become your customer and then buy from you. Look again at figure 6.4, and you'll see that this Window of Dissatisfaction (the dark shaded area) is far too removed from the light shaded area, which represents the area where decision-makers would buy from you.

Although our credibility is increasing over time, the buyer's desire to act is decreasing, as is our opportunity to capitalize on the dissatisfaction with the Status Quo. Our dilemma is clear. We need to get the intersection point of the buyer's intent to act and our credibility above the blue line where the buyer is dissatisfied with the current supplier or solution (the dark shaded area in the curve).

We need get into the dark shaded area in figure 6.4, which represents the Window of Dissatisfaction. This is where we need to be. But how do we get there?

6.4 GETTING INTO THE WINDOW OF DISSATISFACTION

When you first start dealing with a decision-maker in the Window of Dissatisfaction, you often lack the credibility to close the sale before the buyer's intent has diminished to the point where they are unlikely to take action right away.

Fortunately, you can effectively shift the Credibility Curve in your favor to maximize the likelihood of making the sale. There are two strategies you can use to get into the Window of Dissatisfaction:

1. Shift the Credibility Curve upward by reducing the perceived risk of becoming your customer.

2. Shift the Credibility Curve left by accelerating the rate at which we become credible in the buyer's eyes.

6.4.1 *Shift the Credibility Curve Up*

Using your Won Sales Analysis, you will have taken advantage of Selective Perception, and will have focused on those people who are likely (in the foreseeable future) to experience a *Trigger Event* that accelerates your sales cycle. With that decision-maker's profile and likely situation in mind, you can take steps to move the Credibility Curve upward, as indicated in figure 6.5. To do that, you'll be using ideas from this chapter, as well as concepts we shared with you in Chapters 4 and 5.

Figure 6.5

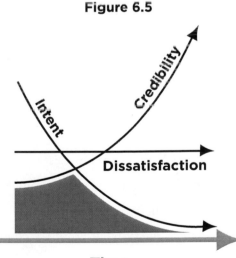

6.4.2 *Shift the Credibility Curve to the Left*

As figure 6.6 shows, we can shift the Credibility Curve to the left by building a relationship with the decision-maker well before the *Trigger Event* occurs. This will ensure that we have some credibility before the event happens.

Figure 6.6

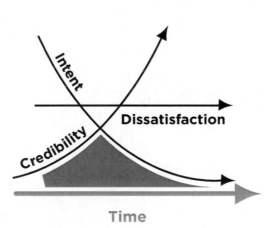

6.4.3 *Do Both!*

Using either strategy on it's own, as you may have noticed, won't always get you into the Window of Dissatisfaction. However, if you employ both of these strategies, you will find yourself looking at a whole new selling landscape: one that eliminates the vast majority of your competitors. It is illustrated in figure 6.7.

Figure 6.7

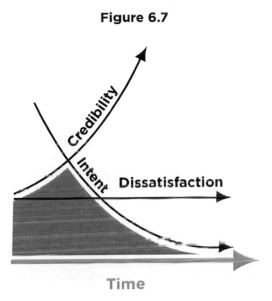

Pursuing Strategy #1 without Strategy #2 is usually not enough. Just reducing the risk does not get you above the Dissatisfaction Line. Just increasing credibility will not get you over the Dissatisfaction Line soon enough.

Time is of the essence when dealing with someone in the Window of Dissatisfaction. If you proceed on both fronts, you are much more likely to be in the Window of Dissatisfaction where the buyer is still motivated to take action, the dissatisfaction is high enough to justify doing so, and your credibility as a seller is sufficient for you to make the sale. It's not just a question of moving the Credibility Curve to the left. You must also move it quickly enough to make it more likely that you will be talking to someone who is dissatisfied, likely to buy, and likely to buy from you.

Got it? Good. You're now ready to look at the two complementary halves of your unified strategy for shifting the Credibility Curve in the right direction... in time for the shift to matter to both you and the buyer.

6.5 SHIFT THE CREDIBILITY CURVE UP

The desired outcome of this strategy is to lower the perceived risk of becoming your customer, which is effectively the same thing as shifting the Credibility Curve up.

To minimize a buyer's perception of the risk of buying from you, you need to understand what constitutes risk. Risk is the multiplication of two elements: complexity and cost.

$$Risk = Complexity \times Cost$$

Complexity is the perceived likelihood that something will go wrong by taking a certain course of action related to your solution—using, installing, or maintaining it.

Cost is the perceived impact if something does go wrong. Think of impact as the financial and political costs to the company and the financial, political, and personal costs to the person who makes the decision.

The higher the potential complexity and potential cost (from the prospect's point of view), the higher the perceived risk.

Consider the following example; Steve uses Local Budget Courier to deliver local packages to his employer's smaller customers (i.e., the ones where there is less of an impact if a late shipment disappoints a customer). He sees that there is limited risk in a shipment being picked up and dropped off by the same vehicle and person, and understands the savings as a benefit with limited offsetting risk.

While Local charges less for delivering to long distance destinations than his usual vendor, National Courier, Steve does not consider switching his long distance shipments or shipments to larger customers to Local Budget Courier.

Why? The potential impact of disappointing a larger customer and the complexity of having packages handled by multiple people during the process of being picked up, tracked, and dropped off is not offset by a large enough discount to take on the additional risk.

When asked about this, Steve points to the fact that National is the vendor of record at his company, and is set up on all their systems. The two companies are connected through Electronic Data Interchange (EDI); at this point, he is satisfied enough with National Courier that it's not worth the time, expense, or effort of getting Local Budget Courier integrated into their existing EDI system.

Notice that Steve's real reasons were based on emotion (risk avoidance) but he justified them using logic (productivity and expenses).

Here's another example. Most of us would not worry about spending $10 to buy a book on Amazon.com using a credit card. If for some reason we don't get the book, we would just phone Amazon and tell them about the problem, and we'd have a reasonable expectation that Amazon would rectify the mistake. If things went off track, and Amazon did not solve our problem, we would simply phone Visa or MasterCard and have the charge taken off our account.

However, would you worry about spending $5 million to buy a seaside home on the cliffs of southern California—using EBay? We could think of many things that could go wrong with that transaction, and the potential impact of those things going wrong could add up to some big problems. If you spend $10 to buy a book online, and something goes wrong, guess what? You lost $10. On the other hand, if you transfer $5 million to buy a home on EBay, you're stuck with a $5 million home that you've never seen, and you're out $5 million.

6.6 RISK AND THE BUYING MODES

Risk is relative to the difference between you and the competition. How risk and competition are perceived varies profoundly, based on the decision-maker's buying mode. To demonstrate, let's look at how decision-makers within each of the three buying modes are likely to perceive risk.

Buying Mode	Status Quo	Window of Dissatisfac-tion	Searching for Alternatives
Competition	Solution they are currently happy with	Solution they are now unhappy with	Other suppliers who sell a similar solution
Risk	All the things that can go wrong by switching solutions now	The potential impact if nothing get done about it	What will happen if they choose the wrong supplier

6.6.1 *Status Quo*

Suppose that you meet a buyer who's in Status Quo buying mode. This person is happy with what they are doing (or not doing). There has been no *Trigger Event*, so this individual's perception of risk is based on the idea of the risk of leaving what they use (which they are currently happy with). People who haven't experienced a *Trigger Event* tend to perceive the act of doing something as the primary risk. Not doing something (that is, not making a decision to purchase your product or service) is the least risky alternative because it is perceived to be safer than changing what appears to be working well enough.

If you determine that this decision-maker has money, authority to spend it, and influence, then you should implement the strategies outlined in Chapter 4 to maximize the likelihood that you get called first when this prospect experiences a *Trigger Event*, moves into the Window of Dissatisfaction, and starts thinking of the risk of staying with what they have.

6.6.2 *Window of Dissatisfaction*

Very different assumptions are in play when you meet someone who's in the Window of Dissatisfaction. This person has recently experienced a *Trigger Event*; their perception of risk is now the risk of inaction, which is the risk of doing nothing. They have now become dissatisfied with what they have and see risk in sticking with the Status Quo.

When you find decision-makers that are in the Window of Dissatisfaction, the risks of staying with the Status Quo are perceived to be high. The risks of being your customer are at their lowest level because the risks of staying with what they have compared to buying from you have shifted significantly in your favor. When you find a decision-maker here, do something about it right now!

There are two reasons that you should not wait to move:

1. The emotion of the *Trigger Event* declines over time. The longer you wait ("longer" is measured in terms of hours and days, not weeks), the less likely you are to fully harness the emotion.

2. The decision-maker who experienced a *Trigger Event* is likely to experience a second or third *Trigger Event*, and then start Searching for Alternatives—without consulting you!

Thus, you must quickly find an opportunity to ask this buyer, "What is the risk of taking more time to make a decision?" (We'll share more insights on this critical sales question for the Window of Dissatisfaction buyer later in this chapter.)

6.6.3 Searching for Alternatives

Another set of circumstances is in play when you meet someone who is in the Searching for Alternatives buying mode. In this case, the *Trigger Event* happened a while ago, and the buyer has been doing something about it for a while. These are the people who ask you for a quote, and have the specifics mapped out already. For this individual, the dominant perception of risk is the risk of taking the wrong action or making the wrong choice.

This is why the Emotional Favorite has such a great position in this buying mode! Ultimately, this prospect is likely to make an emotionally driven decision to work with the person who appears most likely to address the problem with the least risk to the decision-maker and/or their long-term career prospects. That is virtually always the supplier who acquired first-mover advantage. Why? Because that seller defined the terms of the solution when the decision-maker was in the Window of Dissatisfaction! Remember that the Emotional Favorite is in place before the buyer thinks about changing. Therefore, the Emotional Favorite is in a position to capture that emotional moment and shape the perception of the solution.

At this point, the buyer's perception of risk is defined by the difference between you and the current supplier of choice—the Emotional Favorite who beat you to the punch and won first-mover advantage. Rather than spending time trying to win the business by applying all the tips, tricks, tactics, and techniques you have been taught, become the buyer's least risky alternative. When their current preferred choice does something to disappoint them, and they become even more risk averse, your position as the least risky alternative become an even more powerful factor to winning the business.

6.7 REDUCE THE RISKS

There are three ways to reduce the perceived risk of buying from you (and shift the Credibility Curve upward):

1. Reduce the perception of the likelihood that something will go wrong.

2. Reduce the potential impact if something does go wrong.

3. Raise the risks of inaction (by staying with the Status Quo).

6.7.1 *Reduce the Likelihood*

There are three ways to lower the perception of the likelihood that something can go wrong during the buying process:

1. **Make sure that the buyer understands how simple it is to learn about, buy, and implement what you are selling.** The prospect's perception of the likelihood that something can go wrong is related to their perception of the complexity involved with your solution. The simpler you make your solution, the less risk the buyer sees in becoming your customer. Start with something simple and layer the complexities over time (just like we did in this book). Don't overwhelm them with a lot of details at the beginning. This means making the solution simple to learn, simple to buy, simple to take delivery on, simple in the process customers must go through, and simple in terms of the outcome customers receive.

2. **Make your offering consistent, predictable, and reliable.** Customers need to see that every time something is delivered, it meets the expectations you shaped by your previous actions. Demonstrate how it worked for other customers and then show how you delivered to that benchmark each and every time. If you cannot demonstrate that, then the prospect will automatically begin to think of the worst-case scenario.

3. **Make your solution flexible.** As a practical matter, that means it is easy to support, easy to enhance, and easy to expand. How easy is your solution to support and maintain? How easy is it to ensure that it will grow with your customer's requirements? Will it last? Your customers are busy people; the last thing they want to do is solve this problem again a year from now.

6.7.2 *Reduce the Impact*

There are three strategies for reducing the prospect's perception of the costs or impact when something goes wrong:

1. **Provide some form of guarantee** so that the buyer perceives that there is little or no risk. Consider the seller who assures you that if you do not reduce your production time by at least X%, they will refund the difference in cost.

2. **Propose the work be done in stages**. This means taking on a small chunk. We don't want to say, "We're going to do it all at once." Why not? Because the buyer will perceive that as being too risky. You want to take on small pieces of the business and let people see that what you're proposing is going down the right path. Once you have a victory under your belt, you can propose the next chunk and the chunk after that. Part of what you are doing is putting the customer in control and providing them with the option of getting out if things are not working to their satisfaction.

3. **Offset the downside**. Whatever the customer's perceived downside, there must be a way to either offset it or demonstrate an upside that makes the potential risk of the downside worth it. For example, in the world of corporate cell phone plans, switching suppliers used to mean getting a new phone number. That changed with the arrival of phone number portability (the ability to keep your cell phone number when you switch suppliers). That left the prospect with the obligation to their current supplier and having to pay penalties based on the length of time left on the contract. What would happen if you agreed to pay part or all of the penalty as a means of elimi-

nating the downside to the buyer? The buyer would get new equipment and a better plan, and you would receive new activations and locked-in residual.

6.7.3 *Raise the Risk of Inaction*

You can also raise the risk of inaction or deciding to act later. Help the buyer to understand the real-world implications of doing nothing and how they can eliminate that risk by taking action now.

To raise the risk of inaction, illustrate the three types of threats associated with failure to act:

1. **Competitive threats**: What would be the risk of a competitor doing something before they do? First-mover advantage means a lot to those who want acquire or keep customers, employees, and shareholders.

2. **Internal threats**: What would be the risk of not being able to act later because they don't' have the time or access to money or resources? Get the prospect to identify the consequences of having to live with what they have for months or years because they don't have the time, money, people, or political capital to do it later.

3. **Environmental threats**: What would happen if you can't do this in the future for legal reasons?

Determine the risk of a change in the business environment that they would not be able to change in the future for regulatory or statutory reasons.

In this case, you cannot make a statement about the impact of inaction. You must ask the prospect to describe what the impact would be to them and the organization if this threat became a reality.

6.8 SHIFT THE CREDIBILITY CURVE LEFT

Now that you understand risk and how to shift the Credibility Curve up by minimizing the buyer's perception of the risk of becoming your customer, you must overcome the remaining risk the buyer sees in becoming your customer.

In our experience, the best way to overcome the risk that remains is to raise the prospect's perception of your credibility, the solution you are selling, and the organization you represent.

Before we begin, it's important to understand the three components of the buyer's perception of your credibility. These three components are:

1. Expertise Credibility

2. Leveraged Credibility

3. Relationship Credibility

Your overall credibility is the sum of the three kinds of credibility.

Credibility =
Expertise Credibility +
Leveraged Credibility +
Relationship Credibility

By understanding and maximizing each component of credibility, you will shift the Credibility Curve to the left and maximize the likelihood of making the sale.

6.8.1 Expertise Credibility

To develop Expertise Credibility, you must get your message out to the public. You can write an article, give a speech, or build your online presence with a blog that enables you to share your insights and observations on areas of special interest to you. Every time you spread your message, you directly or indirectly help to enhance your Expertise Credibility with prospective buyers.

The more often you speak or write, and the higher the prestige of the location you (or others in your organization) publish articles or speak to audiences, the more Expertise Credibility you will develop. Expertise Credibility will also be magnified if you have multiple subject matter experts in your organization. If you don't have the ability to speak at industry events, then invite customers and prospects to attend webinars and seminars.

6.8.2 *Leveraged Credibility*

To obtain Leveraged Credibility, you need to leverage the name of a person or an entity that the decision-maker trusts.

Leveraged Credibility is created when you are referred by, associated with, or recommended by, someone who has credibility with the decision maker. It can also be created by having a trusted entity sell, install or maintain your solution.

The classic example of Leveraged Credibility is a potential buyer saying, "Craig suggested I give you a call." This is one reason why Trigger Event Referrals (as discussed in Chapter 5) are so powerful.

Leveraged Credibility can also take the form of a title. Where possible, you want to use the credibility of the title attached to your CEO, VP of Sales, or other people in your organization who accompany you on important sales calls.

When Craig used to work at WorldCom, Vint Cerf (hailed as the father of the Internet) was the Senior Vice President of Internet Architecture and Technology: Craig made sure that this piece of information did not go unnoticed by the decision-makers he spoke with.

In general, decision-makers trust the person or organization that refers, sells, installs, and/or supports the product. So the more they know about the credibility of these people or companies, the more Leveraged Credibility you will have.

Leveraged Credibility can enhance your Expertise Credibility by publishing your articles in recognized publications or doing webinars and seminars with recognized experts. Having your CEO or other people from your organization share the stage with a recognized expert is an example of how you can create Leverage Credibility.

6.8.3 *Relationship Credibility*

Relationship Credibility is the most powerful form of credibility. The challenge is that it usually takes the longest time to build. Fortunately, there are some simple steps you can take to accelerate your Relationship Credibility.

For instance, whenever you talk to someone new, find a way to make small commitments, and then follow through on them exactly as promised to prove that you are reliable. If you're talking to a potential account, don't close the call by saying, "Okay, I'll phone you back later." Instead, say, "Can I phone you back in a month? How's the 23rd at 3 PM?" Once you phone back in a month at the stated time, you will begin to establish Relationship Credibility. The only challenge is your level of reliability compared with someone who says, "I will phone you on the third Wednesday of every month." We've had several successes where we've closed the first discussion by saying, "I'll be here the first Wednesday of every month" or "I'll be here every other Tuesday." Following through on those commitments accelerated our Relationship Credibility!

Another good strategy is finding a way to be more familiar. Try to be in the same places as the person you are focusing on so that your name comes up regularly, and they see your face and hear your name in different places. That will help you to become far more familiar.

In the end, accelerating Relationship Credibility is about three things:

1. When you spend time with your contact, what is your motive? Your motive must always be to make the other person look good.

2. Before you actually get the business, are you looking for creative ways to solve problems in this person's world? Remember that you should be willing to employ resources and information that may be completely unrelated to what you sell.

3. When your contact gives you a problem, do you take complete ownership of that problem? Are you out to prove that your contact only has to make one call to one person (you) to be absolutely certain that the problem gets solved?

Relationship Credibility takes some time to build, but probably not as much time as you think. Once you have established

Relationship Credibility, you will find it much easier to establish yourself in the role of Emotional Favorite. Your close ratio will go up, and the price at which you can sell will go up, too.

SHIFT!

There are three key things to take away from this chapter:

1. **THE BIGGEST KILLER OF SALES IS** that the buyer's perception of the risk of buying from you is greater than their perception of your credibility.

2. **YOU MINIMIZE THE RISK OF BECOMING YOUR CUSTOMER BY** reducing the likelihood that something can go wrong and/or the potential impact if it does go wrong.

3. **THE THREE TYPES OF CREDIBILITY ARE** Expertise Credibility, Leverage Credibility, and Relationship Credibility.

Action

To make the most of what you now know, you should do the following:

1. Write articles for industry magazines and speak at industry events to develop your expertise credibility

2. Build relationships with and get referred by those who have as customers those you want as customers to create leveraged credibility.

3. Build relationships with those who have money, authority, and influence before they experience a *Trigger Event* so you can create relationship credibility.

4. **Read the above three point a again because if you execute effectively on the above three you virtually eliminate any resistance to becoming your customer**

Resources

- A full sized (8.5 X 11) version and a completed example of the Credibility Curve worksheet can be downloaded from www. TriggerEventBook.com/credibility

- Special offers and information on Sales 2.0 tools and services that are related to the Credibility Curve can be found at www.TriggerEconomy.com

CHAPTER 7

First Call Effectlveness™

*"When it comes to the future, there are three kinds of people:
those who let it happen, those who make it happen,
and those who wonder what happened."*

~JOHN M. RICHARDSON, JR

A large number of the deals you chase are won or lost on the first call simply berceuse you failed to prevent the series of events that caused a decision maker to start the process of Searching for Alternatives.

Now that you have learned the first six major components of Trigger Event Selling™, it's time to put them all together to make the most of your efforts during your first call (in person or on the phone) to the prospect and prevent, or delay, them from calling your competition. A process we call First Call Effectiveness™

If you don't read this chapter, you will miss out on the following:

1. Identifying which opportunities you are most likely to close

2. Starting prospects down the path of becoming your customer

3. Preventing prospects from noticing and talking to your competition

---

7.1 MAKE THE MOST OF THE FIRST CALL

James sells an accounts receivable application that allows customers to move to a paperless invoicing system. He recently completed a comprehensive Won Sales Analysis encompassing his last two years' worth of wins.

James learned the following about the business that he wins:

- James' deals take an average of eight weeks and four meetings to close if he meets a prospect within two weeks of that person experiencing a *Trigger Event*.

- On the other hand, the process of closing the deal takes ten to twelve weeks and six meetings if he gets to the prospect three to six weeks after a *Trigger Event*

- His chances of closing diminish to almost nothing eight weeks after a *Trigger Event*.

James learned the following about how to make the most of his critical first call with prospects:

- Whenever he starts the process with a Chief Financial Officer or VP of Finance, first meetings that end with getting permission to spend half an hour with the front line accounts receivable person, conduct a template review of the accounts receivable process, and schedule a follow-up meeting with the CFO result in a proposal 90% of the time. Of the proposals generated from such meetings, the value of the deals that close is at over 90% of the initial dollars proposed.

- When James only manages to spend time with the accounts receivable person or do the audit, but not both before meeting with the CFO, he only generates a proposal 70% of the time. These deals close around 80% of the initial dollars proposed.

- When James is only able to get a first and second meeting with the CFO, and does nothing else, he only goes to proposal 45% of the time. The closing rate on this group of discussions is 60% lower than the closing rate of his ideal scenario, and deals usually close from 60% to 80% of the dollar value of the initial proposal. To achieve the price concessions typically required in these scenarios, James usually removes important features, which means that these deals also result in features concessions that may create a weaker Status Quo when James' application becomes the incumbent.

As a result of conducting this detailed analysis of more than 25 closed deals, James knows that the more new CFOs he talks to, and the newer the CFO, the higher his close rate. He now knows—with a great deal of certainty—that he wants to achieve three goals in his initial meetings with a CFO:

1. Meet with the CFO as soon as possible after the *Trigger Event* of the CFO stepping into their new job.

2. Get a commitment for an interview with a frontline user (an audit).

3. Schedule a follow-up meeting with the CFO.

James used the Won Sales Analysis to identify his ideal sales process. With the right people in the conversation, all the relevant facts on the table, and the chance to work quickly to assess the severity of the situation, James can lead a discussion on the impact on the CFO's business, the impact of action, and the potential consequences of not taking action now. As a result of this Won Sales Analysis, James knows exactly how his initial meeting with a CFO should conclude.

7.1.1 *James' Model in Action*

To follow is James' model in action on his first call with Tom, a CFO who started with his new company ten days ago.

James: *Tom, here is what I recommend we do now. The issues and objectives you discussed are things we help clients with every day. In fact, when you are ready, I can put you in touch with some of them. But right now what I recommend is that you let Charlotte know that I will be calling her to set up a time to talk with her and record an interview. When I meet with her I can also conduct our A/R Reveal Audit. Actually, now that I think of it, do you want Charlotte to help with this, or should I work with Harvey?*

Tom: *Talk to Harvey. He is involved with a number of other areas, so he could give you better input.*

James: *Great. If you can give me their contact information now, I can call from my car when I leave and set things up. I'll make sure that I get all that done by Friday. Why don't you and I schedule a lunch for next week? Then I can tell you what I learned, how that fits with what I learned from you today, and then I will present the proposal I believe can help you achieve the objectives you outlined today. How about lunch next Tuesday?*

(Did you notice James getting Tom out of his office, away from the interruptions of phone calls, e-mails, subordinates, superiors, and peers? Did you notice that he made a time commitment of wrapping up the interview with Harvey by Friday? It is now mandatory that James complete that deliverable in the timeframe he promised. If he doesn't, he will lose precious credibility.)

Tom: *Sounds like a good plan. I'll send an e-mail to Harvey and Charlotte later today and copy you.*

James: *Can we do it now?*

Tom: *Sure.*

(Did you notice that James does not walk out of the meeting without getting access to the key people needed for the next phase of his sales cycle? He knows that while Tom has great intentions of e-mailing Harvey and Charlotte later today, as soon as James leaves the meeting Tom is highly likely to get distracted by other action items or interrupted by someone, and the e-mail will not get sent for a day or two. This would lead to the audit not happening until a week later, and Tom's travel schedule would cause the lunch to be rescheduled for three weeks out. By that time, a different *Trigger Event* means that something else will become Tom's priority and the deal will die before there is a second meeting.)

James: *Great. So I'll talk to Harvey by Friday, and share what I learn and a proposal at our lunch next Tuesday.*

7.1.2 **The Best Plan**

James has just executed his best plan for the first call, based on his Won Sales Analysis. Assuming that James did some fact finding about how Tom's organization makes decisions and who else needs to be involved, James has ensured that the prospect is emotionally committed to his solution and is not likely to phone the competition. In fact, James has created a situation where even if a competitor did phone Tom, that competitor would be likely to face a Status Quo type of response.

Tom had the opportunity to tell James that he would just discuss his findings on Tuesday, but he agreed to go beyond that. He agreed to discuss James' proposal. This is usually a very emotional event for both parties. It's now on Tom's radar screen!

Tom will follow up with Charlotte and Harvey. Assuming

that James does his usual professional job, he will have created new relationships with people who will boost his Leveraged Credibility when Tom asks them how things went. The audit will boost James's Expertise Credibility, as it has impressed most Finance Managers or Comptrollers like Harvey.

7.2 REPEAT, REPEAT, REPEAT

At the start of the book, we asked you to write your name repeatedly with the hand you don't normally use for writing. Beyond highlighting the discomfort associated with doing something we have mastered in a new way, we wanted you to embrace was the notion of repetition.

Since that point, we have introduced a number of important concepts and related practices to help you recognize and act on opportunities to improve your timing when engaging with highly motivated decision-makers who are likely to make a purchasing decision in the near future. Now it is time to pull all these elements together and help you take action on them in your world. If repetition paves the road to success (and it does), we want to get you started with a process that you can start repeating—a series of sequential steps you can execute in a logical fashion on that all-important first meeting. The more closely those steps align with what you have learned from your Won Sales Analysis, of course, the better off you will be.

You must fully harness *Trigger Events* and continuously

improve your timing and interactions with prospects and clients. The effectiveness of your first call is crucial to your success, as well as the speed and size, of your sale.

By the end of a successful first meeting, you must be in the same position that James enjoyed. Specifically, you must:

- Be able to rank the opportunity as something worthy of continued effort.

- Start the decision-maker down the path of becoming your customer, which creates Path Dependency around you and your solution.

- Turn off the decision-maker's Selective Perception so that they will stop noticing other ways to solve the problem and be far less likely to talk to your competitor than before the next meeting.

7.3 TRIGGER EVENT QUALIFYING™

The best way to sell more is to spend more time on deals that you are most likely to close (and less time on those deals you are unlikely to close). This seems obvious, but most salespeople spend their most precious resource (time) chasing deals that are highly unlikely to close. They could (and should) make better use of their precious time by prospecting for new deals that match the profile of the deals that are most likely to close. To do that, however, they need a highly effective process for qualifying the deals that are already in their pipeline.

This process is called Trigger Event Qualifying™.

The intent is to give each opportunity you chase a score from 1 to 10. This is not a prediction of the likelihood you will close a deal but rather a deal-ranking mechanism. It allows you to rank the deals you are currently pursuing according to the prospect's likelihood of buying from you.

Figure 7.1

Trigger Event Selling™

Trigger Event Qualifying™

Success Predictor	"2"	"1"	"0"
1			
2			
3			
4			
5			

Template produced in cooperation with Strategico Marketing Group

7.3.1 How to Qualify You Opportunities

Select and rank your top five success predictors. As illustrated in figure 7.1, we have provided five examples of good success predictors. The ones you choose are likely to be tied more specifically to your world and the specific findings of your Won Sales Analysis.

Once you have identified and ranked your success predictors, organize them as follows:

- Best case scenario (below the column labeled "2")

- Conservative scenario (below the column labeled "1")

- Worst case scenario (below the column labeled "0")

When you come across a new opportunity, there are three things you should do:

1. Assign a best case, conservative case, or worst case rating for each of the five success factors.

2. Rate the opportunity by adding the scores for each of your success factors.

3. Work this opportunity based on how its rating compares to your other opportunities, starting with your highest scoring opportunities first.

When there is a tie, work on opportunities according to the highest score on the first criteria. If there is still a tie, move to the next criteria and work on the highest scoring.

For example, if you have five opportunities that you ranked a seven, then work on those that have the highest score on Buying Mode. If you have three opportunities that you ranked a seven, and in all three cases the decision-maker is in the

Window of Dissatisfaction, look at their scores in the *Trigger Event* type (Bad Experience, Change/Transition, Awareness). If you are then left with two opportunities that have the same scores, then move to Time From *Trigger Event* and work the opportunity with the highest score in that success factor.

Now you have all your opportunities ranked in likelihood of closing according to the criteria and scenarios that came from your Won Sales Analysis. Choose the right strategy based upon their buying mode. Remember to use the material in each chapter to overcome the weaknesses in your credibility and risk scores.

7.4 START THEM DOWN YOUR PATH

If you don't get a prospect far enough down the path of becoming your customer, they may stop, back up, and switch paths. When initiating an opportunity, your goal is to get the prospect far enough down the path of buying from you that their emotional energy for investigating a competitor's solution diminishes to the point where they don't give your competitors the same amount of time or effort that you received. This will make it very difficult for a competitor to win the business.

You may have an intuitive sense of what will help you to win this type of emotional engagement from the prospective buyer.

If you work for a software company, it may involve a demonstration for the CEO. If you work for a trucking or logistics company, it may mean a tour of your facilities conducted by a senior person in your company.

You want these types of events to happen as soon as possible— when the decision-maker is still high on the curve of diminishing intent and they have not yet had contact with your competitors. Very often, a decision-maker will only visit one or two companies before finalizing a short list. After that, decision-makers often conclude that bringing others into the conversation "isn't worth the effort." **You want to be on the short list of people they visit, meet with, or try out.**

For example, salespeople with an office furniture distributor have been taught to get potential customers to fill out a credit application during the first call. In doing so, they set themselves up for success when a customer chooses a product that has a lead time greater than the time they need the office furniture. The prospect no longer has the time or inclination to complete and wait for the approval of a credit application with a competitor.

Once you understand the decision-maker's expectations in terms of a solution, you can start planting seeds about how what you sell can do exactly that. You can make it more likely that the decision-maker will conclude that there are no significant gaps between what they want and what you have. You have effectively turned off Selective Perception.

Now the decision-maker is much less likely to notice all the ways of solving this problem, and more likely to notice all the ways what you sell can add value to their role and business.

7.5 GETTING STARTED

As you now know, to maximize the impact of your first call, you must first determine a prospect's current buying mode: Status Quo, Searching for Alternatives, or Window of Dissatisfaction.

It will not always be easy to determine a prospect's buying mode. If a client calls to tell you that they are looking for a solution and would like to include your offering in their quest, you know that they are Searching for Alternatives. You may get a referral from a friend that his cousin Jake may be interested in your service. After three calls, Jake agrees to see you "because Steve is my cousin and I owe him one," which makes it likely that Jake is comfortably in Status Quo mode. You may call a prospect the same morning that the system crashed for the third time in less than a month, and he acknowledges that he doesn't think his boss will allow him to survive another crash in short order. You know that you are dealing with someone in the Window of Dissatisfaction, having just experienced a *Trigger Event* or two. But clear examples like these are the exception, not the rule.

You usually have to spend some time and effort to figure out a given prospect's buying mode. While there is no perfect way, there are some things you can do to vastly improve your odds of categorizing the prospect, and then acting and executing accordingly.

7.6 PROCESS OF ELIMINATION

We strongly recommend using a methodology that allows you to eliminate the two buying modes that buyers are not in; as you do that, you will be left with the mode they are in. Most salespeople will look for "positives" and then, based on their interpretation of those clues, decide which mode "looks best." This is not a practical way to go; people who use this technique usually don't hit the right buying mode on the first try. All too often, they give overoptimistic assessments based on their emotions, not the buyer's emotions, and end up trying to force a square peg into a round hole.

Here your role model is Sherlock Holmes: you want to logically eliminate options, rather than make an immediate, and perhaps impulsive, assumption about what's going on. Of course, there will be situations when you know for certain that someone is in a specific buying mode, as in the "Steve is my cousin" example. That's nice when it happens but we're interested in what happens most of the time. The process of eliminating the modes the buyer is not in is significantly more accurate than focusing on positive cues and going with the wrong mode.

To use this process of elimination, you must learn what has recently happened in this person's world. Does it look unfamiliar, based on the Won Sale Analysis you have conducted? You can only answer this question if you have the courage to focus on your wins, as we showed you how to do in Chapter 3, and then eliminate everything that does not match that pattern. (You certainly don't want to waste time trying to sell to people who are in Status Quo or Searching for Alternatives modes.)

It's important to understand that "eliminate" does not mean banish from your memory or delete from your database. Today's loss could be tomorrow's win. Eliminate means to question the timing by asking, "Is now the right time to work with XYZ Inc.?" If the answer is yes, then get to it. If not, then move on; as circumstances change, XYZ Inc. will change too, and may well move into the Window of Dissatisfaction, which means the timing will have changed. This is why we place such heavy emphasis on identifying those people for whom you want to become the Emotional Favorite. When the timing changes, you can re-engage with the decision-maker with whom it makes the most sense for you to invest your time, effort, and energy.

If someone you want to work with hasn't experienced a *Trigger Event*, then the question becomes what *Trigger Events* to look for and how to best to leverage them in the future. Eliminate as much noise and distraction as possible so that you can focus on those opportunities with the greatest likelihood of closing based on timing, not luck or pure numbers.

Many salespeople have difficulty identifying the prospects

they should not be spending time with. Instead, they do what is familiar, which involves spending time with anyone who will talk to them. The reality—which we must compensate for—is that as salespeople we can always rationalize why something "looks good." We are less likely to stay invested when things don't "look good." The simplest way to achieve this is to ask specific questions to help you assess where they are not.

To begin, you must understand how the market generally breaks down using the three buying modes. The largest of the three groups is Status Quo mode, which, depending on your industry, includes 75% to 90% of the market at any given time. This means that most of the people you're eliminating fall into this group. The smallest group is Searching for Alternatives, which constitutes 5% to 10% of the market. The group making up the Window of Dissatisfaction sits in the middle, with about 5% to 15% of the market.

Experience has shown that the most difficult group to correctly pinpoint consists of people in Window of Dissatisfaction mode. This is why we must set out to eliminate people from the other two modes, which are easier to identify.

7.7 WHAT TO ASK

The following questions, which should ideally be asked before your first extended meeting, can help in the elimination process. It is not an exhaustive list, but it will allow you to engage in a conversation where you can ascertain a buyer's mode without closing the door to future opportunities. These questions are starting points to an early conversation with any prospective buyer.

7.7.1 *What Are You Doing Now?*

You want to know how they are currently addressing, dealing with, or managing the process or issue in question. Beyond the factual data you will capture, you will also get a clear sense of how much the person has invested in the current solution (Status Quo), as well as what is needed to change the path they are currently on. The more thought, time, and resources they are spending on changing the issue, the less likely they are in Status Quo. On the other hand, if a buyer seems surprised by the question "How are you handling X?", it would suggest that the person has not paid much attention to the situation, and is happy with things as they are.

7.7.2 *How Is Your Relationship With Your Current Supplier?*

What does the buyer like about the current provider? If a buyer speaks glowingly about a provider, then they are likely in Status Quo.

Warning: If a buyer finds it difficult to come up with nice things to say about the current provider, it may not mean that they are in the Window of Dissatisfaction. The buyer may not have given the issue much thought because the relationship is working and they have other things to think about.

7.7.3 How, When, and Why Did You Pick Your Current Provider?

"How" will give you the objective side of the buy. "Why" will reveal the emotional approach. "When" will tell you about the history (and duration) of the relationship. These three lines of questioning will tell you a lot about the situation; combined with intelligence from your Won Sales Analysis. Answers to these questions will go a long way toward telling you how entrenched the current supplier is. By understanding how the organization went about selecting the current provider, you will not only learn about the selection criteria but also the organizational decision-making and buying process. While specs and factors will change over time, habits don't. (Note: Asking "how," "why," and "when" questions will often reveal *who* was involved in the purchasing decision more effectively than asking the "who" question directly.)

7.7.4 What Would You Be Doing about This if I Had Not Contacted You?

If the buyer reels off a bunch of initiatives that they have already put in motion relating to this issue, then they are definitely not in Status Quo. Your next job is to explore how far down the road the person has gone. If the buyer has moved from consideration to selection, you know that they are in Searching for Alternatives mode. If the buyer has to think and reflect as to what would have happened if you had not called, then you can eliminate Searching for Alternatives and move to validating that the person is in Status Quo.

7.8 SECOND-LEVEL QUESTIONING

You will often have to drill further to confirm things and not be misled by false indications. You should go beyond the facts and test the implications of the initial answers. What may seem like Status Quo mode could be someone who has moved into the Window of Dissatisfaction, but is unwilling to disclose this to you yet. In many ways, this is good (almost optimal) timing, but it is often missed when people rely on one initial response. If people continue to hold their cards close to the vest when you ask "how" and "why" questions, you can usually eliminate the Window of Dissatisfaction and Searching for Alternatives modes. Assume that you are talking to someone in Status Quo.

At other times, you may realize that you are working with someone who knows the Status Quo is no longer viable, and has recently experienced a *Trigger Event*. The issue you've raised may not yet be high enough on the priority list to motivate the buyer, especially if the buyer feels that if they address other aspects of their process, doing so will also address the issue in question. In other words, the initial *Trigger Event* happened a while ago, and either a different *Trigger Event* made something else more of a priority or your contact perceived the effort required to make change to be too much at this time. Again, the best way to ensure that you are interpreting their feedback correctly and pursuing the right opportunities based on timing is to go below the surface level indications of the first response.

Examine your Won Sales Analysis and determine the effect of the *Trigger Events*. What other aspects of the buyer's process were being influenced directly or indirectly, and how? You can then use those answers to develop validation questions. By developing these secondary questions, you can efficiently find the buyer's current mode by eliminating the modes they are currently not in.

7.9 PREPARING FOR A FIRST CALL

Having looked at how to determine the prospect's buying mode through the process of elimination, we'll examine how the elements and techniques discussed in this book come together to create an Effective First Meeting. Let's look at how this could work in real-life selling situations.

What follows is an outline of a deal that came together as a result of a number of events and people's actions that created an opportunity to leverage and benefit from a specific *Trigger Event*. That event triggered a number of related events. That first domino put into action a series of other events.

We always disliked books that illustrate complex sales scenarios using an example of Baba selling a widget in a one horse town. (That's not what you sell, right?) Since we are basing this on real life, there are a number of moving parts, moving in parallel but different pace and rhythm. Many of you will recognize it right away; others may have to read it two or three times. We encourage you to read it until you can not only see all the moving pieces, but you can see how moving one will impact the other or how moving one the right way at the right time can win you the deal.

7.9.1 *The Sellers*

There are four parties involved in this scenario:

1. **Helen** works as a salesperson for a recruiting company.

2. **Peter** is a salesperson for an online CRM system provider.

3. **Patti** is an organizational design consultant.

4. **George** represents a major wireless communications provider.

You can see how they are currently connected to each other via the network map in figure 7.2.

Figure 7.2

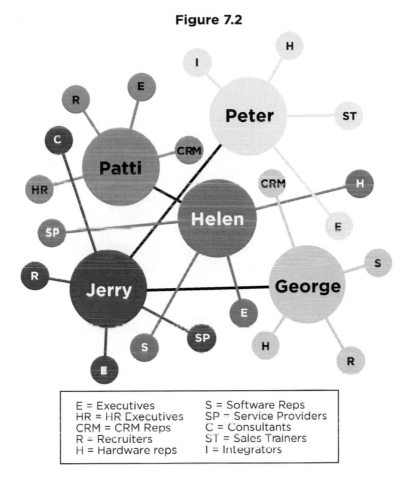

E = Executives   S = Software Reps
HR = HR Executives   SP = Service Providers
CRM = CRM Reps   C = Consultants
R = Recruiters   ST = Sales Trainers
H = Hardware reps   I = Integrators

7.9.2 Helen's Story

Meet Helen Fraser, Account Manager at Blue Box Staffing, a full service staffing and recruitment company that offers a full range of services to multiple verticals. Her company's services include temporary staffing, temp-to-hire staffing, contract staffing, direct hire staffing, executive search, onsite management, outplacement, and payrolling. Helen specializes in Finance and IT; in addition to managing existing client relationships, she works with candidates and prospects for new companies. Due to the demanding nature of Helen's role, and the fact that she can only spend 30% of her time in new business acquisition mode (i.e., prospecting and selling any given deal), maximizing her time is an absolute must.

Due to the nature of the industry, Helen needs to prospect across the board, with many prospects who already have standing relationships with other staffing firms; some of these relationships are transactional, and some are contractual. As in other industries, many transactional situations are built on long-standing relationships. Helen's market provides many opportunities for leveraging timing, new perspectives, and *Trigger Events*.

Helen regularly conducts a Won Sales Analysis, which not only helps Helen to improve her Selective Perception but also helps her to create and execute a plan for each prospect. By mapping out her ideal sales process, Helen has a clear objective for each encounter. Her ability to achieve those objectives helps her to decide who continues to merit her time and effort, based on the likelihood of achieving each incremental step. Armed with this knowledge and action plan, Helen can set her "process of elimination" objectives for each discussion.

Helen heard that FlexCorp, a mid-sized office equipment company that had never bought from her before, had a number of mission critical projects on the go. FlexCorp had just made the decision to roll out a new Customer Relationship Management (CRM) program for their national sales team. She learned of this initiative (which would replace or upgrade the existing CRM system) from Peter, a CRM sales rep, with whom Helen had done work in the past.

Helen knew that companies that had rolled out this CRM usually integrated the system into the company's Enterprise Resource Planning (ERP) software. She also knew that both CRM providers FlexCorp was considering would require the company to upgrade its current ERP. She knew from her Won Sales Analysis, research, and experience that the decision to upgrade the ERP package lags behind the CRM rollout by five months. Both the CRM rollout and ERP work typically required project management help and contract IT people.

Currently, Helen knew only the names and titles of two key figures at FlexCorp: Brenda Hope, CTO, and Bob Nelson, the director heading the CRM project. She also knew that Blue Box Staffing had placed some people for a project at FlexCorp last year. At the time, a sales rep (who was no longer with Blue Box Staffing) had worked on that project; all indications were that key managers at FlexCorp had been impressed with the people and project managers provided by Blue Box Staffing.

Helen had a working relationship with Peter, the CRM sales rep, whom she had met during an earlier project. In fact, Helen had referred Peter to a few of her clients looking to implement a CRM, which brought Helen a lot of valuable information from Peter's side about FlexCorp. Peter knew that FlexCorp would need top-notch contractors to ensure on-time implementation and rollout.

Once Helen was aware that Peter was a finalist, she knew that she would need to connect with a good ERP sales rep to create an opportunity for a two-way referral. She knew that Peter could open the door for her to meet either or both the CTO and the director on the CRM project. Her plan was to leverage Peter's relationship with the buyer, reduce perceived risk, establish credibility, and begin the process of becoming the Emotional Favorite. The second part of Helen's plan was to meet an ERP rep who could eventually be helpful to FlexCorp director's when they will require to make decisions about the ERP upgrade, one specifically Peter has also worked with. By introducing the ERP rep to FlexCorp at the right time, Helen can establish herself as an Emotional Favorite with the Flex-Corp director, and also create an opportunity where she could cement her status as the ERP rep's Emotional Favorite and create future reciprocation opportunities.

Helen knew that two potential risk issues were complexity and cost. She felt that she could leverage two factors to address these issues. On the cost side, she knew that late completion of the project would create greater cost than the perceived incremental premium often associated with pricing. To manage or negate the complexity, she planned to leverage her relationship with Peter, who had worked with several contractors she had placed. She knew that these contractors were familiar with Peter's application and that he would look good as a result of their work.

7.9.3 Peter's Story

As mentioned earlier, Helen reached this point because she received a call from Peter, who told her that he was in the running at FlexCorp. Let's look at Peter's situation.

Peter's CRM company is recognized as one of the top players, having a flexible offering that can be installed locally or used on demand, but it is not the leading provider. Over the years, Peter has learned from his Won Sales Analysis that new VPs of Sales tend to make bold changes in their first six months on the job. One of the most common is the decision to either bring on a new CRM or expand an existing CRM system. These changes tend to launch near the end of the first six months of the VP's tenure.

Peter constantly monitors movement of VPs of Sales from one company to another. His aim is to track those he has relationship credibility with so that he can engage them should they move. He also tracks others (using business networking sites such as LinkedIn) for insights on companies where he may be able to gain new business. The challenge Peter faces with VPs is that he does not know how to get in front of them in the right time-frame and demonstrate adequate credibility in the (short) time that precedes their decision to launch a new CRM initiative.

Over the years, Peter has noticed that there is a group of consultants that tends to be engaged by organizations looking to change their go-to-market and/or sales culture or approach. Often, these consultants are rooted in Human Resources and are on the scene before the new VP of Sales is recruited. The moment he realized this, Peter began attending events where these consultants were either presenting or likely to be in the audience.

Peter also learned from his Won Sales Analysis that those consultants who dealt with process and workflow issues tended to rely more heavily on CRM applications to drive the process. They would inevitably recommend either the acquisition of a CRM or major overhauls to the existing system. His Won Sales Analysis revealed that one challenge he would have to overcome was the perceived cost benefit of revamping a competitor's existing CRM system (or replica).

As a result of these insights, Peter spent more time looking for and interacting with consultants whose specialties included sales process and workflow, and who targeted businesses with multiple locations and a dispersed sales force. His Won Sale Analysis had shown him that by targeting VPs of Sales who work with these consultants, he could emphasize standardization, Peter's key deliverable.

Beyond the consultants, Peter tries to build relationships with people who sell hardware (specifically servers for new projects), recruiters of sales teams, or people like Helen who can make Peter look good in multiple ways. He also spends time with sales trainers as a means of leveraging their networks.

Peter often faces the regular challenge of credibility, which has a double impact within his target prospect group. One was a new VP of Sales' general lack of familiarity with Peter; the second was the widespread feeling among these prospects that they only have so much risk capital, and their resulting propensity to be influenced by a "we can build it here" from the internal IT organization. This type of environment virtually always leads to curtailed deals.

Winning a referral from a consultant who could introduce Peter to a VP of Sales helped him to fully utilize and benefit from Leverage Credibility, but it was only a start. To take it further, Peter made it a practice to collect testimonials from every account he won and had completed a Won Sales Analysis for. This helped him to demonstrate Expertise Credibility without "preaching." Simultaneously, this tactic helped him to enhance Relationship Credibility with VPs of Sales he had worked with in the past.

7.9.4 *Patti's Story*

One of the consultants that Peter knows is Patti Carter. Patti is an organizational design consultant who specializes in the design, implementation, and evaluation of smart, innovative human capital strategy. She works with large corporations looking to outsource specific HR needs, such as staffing and placement strategies, the resolution of employee relations issues, management development programs, and a variety of training and compliance programs. She also handles executive recruiting.

Not too long ago, Patti called Peter to tell him about the work she was doing at FlexCorp. She passed along information about a new VP of Sales, since she knew that this was something Peter always wants to hear about. Patti had told Peter that FlexCorp had hired Jerry Brite as its new VP of Sales. Jerry had been in the office equipment business for some time, and FlexCorp was happy to sign him because of his stellar reputation. Based on Patti's focus on process and workflow, and Jerry's reputation for modernizing and leveraging technology for efficiency gains, Patti felt that Peter should meet Jerry.

7.9.5 *Peter's Emotional Favorite Status*

As luck would have it, Peter had a couple of regional office equipment clients. One of those clients worked with Jerry Brite at Xerox about 11 years ago. This person still had contact with Jerry at industry events, and was happy to be a referral for Jerry, who was his Emotional Favorite in the world of CRM applications.

As you'll see in a moment, Peter's Won Sales Analysis made it possible to create that Emotional Favorite relationship. It also helped him create the opportunity at FlexCorp and made it possible to be in a position to help Helen.

7.9.6 *Jerry's Mission*

Jerry Brite, the new VP of Sales at FlexCorp, is an industry veteran, having worked for a number of major office equipment manufacturers and distributors over 25 years. Before he went into management, Jerry was a great salesperson; his charisma and outgoing personality made him a natural sales leader. He loved closing deals, and when he became a sales manager, he loved to reward his reps whenever they closed a big deal. Jerry was always looking for some edge that would help him to boost his (and his team's) performance, and he was a fan of using technology as a competitive advantage. Jerry realized that a new CRM system could give FlexCorp that kind of edge.

Jerry was a proponent of streamlining process, communication, and workflow. He was also a proponent of "the mobile sales office." He felt that a sales rep should be able to get what they need anywhere—and should always have the resources necessary to move a deal forward without having to return to the office. When he came to FlexCorp, he noticed that only senior management had smartphones; front line managers and reps were still depending on low-functionality phones, PC-based order systems, and out-of-date collateral. Jerry resolved to get smartphones for everyone on the sales team, and to provide applications for order processing, credit check, and CRM functions. The current CRM used by FlexCorp did not support these features.

Jerry also knew that the CRM rollout had to be as seamless as possible, as he wanted people to focus on the process and outcome, not on technology glitches.

7.9.7 *George's Story*

Jerry went to his go-to wireless sales rep (Emotional Favorite) George, whom he had worked with on two other CRM rollouts over the last three years, each resulting in a measured improvement in sales and ROI on the smartphone investment.

Because sales teams were about 30% of George's base, he was also familiar with CRM sales reps; they were a natural source of referrals. George knew Peter. His company had used Blue Box in the past, but he did not know Helen.

After meeting with Jerry and Patti, George had pointed out that the current CRM would not support Jerry's plans. Patti agreed with George; she had told Jerry that he should meet with Peter.

George said, "I know Peter. We just did a wireless order entry system at a trucking firm. We were already doing their asset tracking, and order entry was a natural extension of the CRM they had in place; it allowed customers to track their orders and shipments."

George also realized, and readied himself for, meeting

ERP reps, knowing that Jerry's plans will require a new CRM. When Peter's CRM is selected, it will require not only hardware upgrades, but an ERP upgrade. Finding reliable ERP salespeople was a new task for George.

7.9.8 Did You Notice What Each Person Did Right?

- Helen created a relationship with someone who knew of projects before she did, and passed along referrals to take advantage of the principle of reciprocation.

- Peter understood that a change in the VP of Sales position often precedes dissatisfaction with the current CRM and creates new opportunity. This is Peter's *Trigger Event*! Peter also started building key relationships early, and positioned himself as the Emotional Favorite once the decision to install a new CRM had been made.

- Patti created a reciprocal lead-swapping relationship with Peter and others.

- George shared the name of a vendor who could make everyone (including himself) look good. He also improved Peter's credibility by reinforcing Patti's recommendation of Peter.

So now you've seen how we get to the meeting by doing the work in advance in the form of consistent Won Sales Analysis, review of results, and constant adjustment based on success factors.

Now the questions to answer include:

- How can you improve your timing and make things happen while the intent to act is still high?

- Having captured first-mover advantage, how can you seize the initiative and ensure that when you leave that *first meeting* (or any meeting) that prospect continues to focus their energy on making this deal happen *with you* and tunes out the competition?

- How do you set and maintain the flow, increasing sales velocity in the process? (Speed is critical because the faster you can make the deal happen, the less time there is for other suppliers to become a factor.)

Answering those kinds of questions is the "art" part of the sale. Your Won Sales Analysis must serve as the "science" part of the sale. It must be a sales compass that quantifiably identifies who you should be talking to, how many calendar days the sales process should take end to end, how many meetings are optimal, what the goal of each meeting should be.

SHIFT!

There are three key things to take away from this chapter:

1. THE OPPORTUNITIES YOU ARE MOST LIKELY TO CLOSE ARE those with the highest score from your Trigger Event Qualifying.

2. PROSPECTS START BECOMING YOUR CUSTOMER WHEN you harness their high level of intent by getting them to take actions now that they are unlikely to take with your competitors once their intention wanes.

3. PROSPECTS ARE LESS LIKELY TO ENGAGE YOUR COMPETITORS WHEN they start seeing themselves using your solution to solve their problem.

Action

To take advantage of what you now know, you should do the following:

1. Conduct a Won Sales Analysis after each and every sales you win.

2. Create a sales plan for your first call with a decision-maker based upon your Won Sales Analysis.

3. Rank every opportunity based upon your completed Trigger Event Qualifying worksheet.

Resources

- A full sized (8.5 X 11) version and a completed example of the Trigger Event Qualifying worksheet can be downloaded from www.TriggerEventBook.com/qualify

- Special offers and information on Sales 2.0 tools and services that are related to the Trigger Event Qualifying can be found at www.TriggerEconomy.com

ABOUT CRAIG ELIAS

Craig Elias is the creator of Trigger Event Selling™, and the Chief Catalyst of *SHiFT* Selling, Inc.

Craig's *Trigger Event* strategies have:

- Won him a $1,000,000 prize in a global "Billion-Dollar Idea" pitch competition

- Made him a top performer at every company he has worked for – Including WorldCom where he was named #1 within 6 months of joining the company

- Earned his last company, the distinction as one of Dow Jones' 50 most promising companies in North America

- Resulted in coverage on NBC news, in The New York Times, The National Post, The Wall Street Journal, Sales and Marketing magazine, and Business 2.0

ABOUT TIBOR SHANTO

A 20-year veteran of the information, content management, and financial sectors, Tibor has developed an insider's perspective on how information can be used to, shorten sales cycles, increase close ratios, and create double digit growth. Called a brilliant sales tactician Tibor shows organizations how to execute their strategy by using the right information to create the perfect combination of what are the tactics to apply and when.

Prior to Renbor, Tibor spent 10 years with Dow Jones; after launching their Canadian business and building a solid team and revenue base, with double digit CAGR, Tibor was appointed Sales Director for Canada and The Central USA. As Director of Sales Strategy, Tibor developed a very forward thinking global Sales Training program and was instrumental in building their Client Solutions organization. Tibor is a director and contributor to The Sales Bloggers Union.